Spiritual Direction From Dante

SPIRITUAL DIRECTION
from
DANTE

AVOIDING THE INFERNO

Paul Pearson of the Oratory

TAN Books
Charlotte, North Carolina

Copyright © 2019 Paul Pearson, C.O.

All rights reserved. With the exception of short excerpts used in articles and critical reviews, no part of this work may be reproduced, transmitted, or stored in any form whatsoever, printed or electronic, without the prior written permission of the publisher.

Unless otherwise noted, Scripture quotations are from the Revised Standard Version of the Bible—Second Catholic Edition (Ignatius Edition), copyright © 2006 National Council of the Churches of Christ in the United States of America. Used by permission. All rights reserved.

Excerpts from the English translation of the Catechism of the Catholic Church for use in the United States of America copyright © 1994, United States Catholic Conference, Inc.—Libreria Editrice Vaticana. Used with permission.

Passages from papal documents, encyclicals, and addresses © Libreria Editrice Vaticana unless otherwise noted. All rights reserved. Used with permission.

Cover design by Caroline K. Green

Cover image: Dante and Virgil beset by demons on their passage through the eighth circle. Illustration (1861) by Gustave Dore for Dante's Inferno. Wood engraving / Universal History Archive/UIG / Bridgeman Images

Interior images by Gustave Dore for Dante's Inferno. Wood engravings / Veneranda Biblioteca Ambrosiana, Milan, Italy / De Agostini Picture Library / and Universal History Archive/UIG / Bridgeman Images

Library of Congress Control Number: 2018962514

ISBN: 978-1-5051-1232-0

Published in the United States by
TAN Books
P.O. Box 410487
Charlotte, NC 28241
www.TANBooks.com

Printed in the United States of America

To the seminarians of Saint Philip's Seminary

CONTENTS

Foreword   xv
Preface   xix
Acknowledgments   xxiii

INTRODUCTION   1

The Inferno

CANTO 1   13
Wandering From the Path
Self-Sabotage in the Spiritual Life
Rejecting Our False Self-Reliance
Learning to Hate Sin

CANTO 2   27
Giving Up Hope That We Can Be Different
Isolation in Our Battle

CANTO 3   38
This Life Is Our Opportunity to Change
Abdicating Our Responsibility
A Principle-Driven Life
The Fatal Attraction of Sin

Canto 4 — 50
God Is at Work in Our Lives
Spiritual Blindness About Our Own Faults
The Potential Goodness of Human Work
Yearning for More Than This World Can Give

Canto 5 — 63
Some Sins Are More Destructive Than Others
The Power of Passion
The Human Tendency to Self-Deception
Our Weakness in the Face of Temptation

Canto 6 — 75
The Beastliness of Undirected Passion
Pitying What We Ourselves Have Experienced
The Holiness of Our Bodies

Canto 7 — 82
Money, the Root of All Evils
The Spiritual Futility of Sin
Detachment, Not Deprivation
The Ferocious Grip of Anger

Canto 8 — 92
Anger, the Door to Unexpected Sins
Battle Against Our Most Besetting Sins
Hell as a Prison
Breaking Through Hardness of Heart

CONTENTS

CANTO 9 — 100
Trust in God as a Last Resort
Our Need for Support in the Spiritual Life
Our Frustrating Lack of Progress
A Humble Heart and a Believing Intellect

CANTO 10 — 109
True Belief as the Guide to Good Action
Our Spiritual Selves
The Stubborn Unwillingness to Admit We Are Wrong
Living in the Present Moment

CANTO 11 — 118
God's Providence at Every Moment
Every Sin's Victim
Truth as a Building Block of Society

CANTO 12 — 128
The Angry Roots of Violence
The Dehumanizing Power of Intimidation

CANTO 13 — 135
The Hiddenness of Human Suffering
Pain as a Cry for Help
The Self-Focus of Suffering
Treating Our Lives as Disposable
The Self-Destructiveness of Financial Irresponsibility

CANTO 14 — 148
Destroying Our Peace of Mind
The Obsessive Call to Disbelief
The By-Products of Evil

Canto 15 — 157
The Holiness of Sexuality
Silence in the Face of Wrong
Sin and Cover-Up

Canto 16 — 165
A Culture of Secrecy
Public Honor and Private Shame

Canto 17 — 171
Fraud and Isolation
Work as an Element of Human Perfection
Trusting as We Step Into the Unknown

Canto 18 — 179
Self-Defensiveness in a Harsh World
Sex and Deception
Using Sex as a Means of Manipulation
Flattery, a Costly Exchange

Canto 19 — 188
Selling What Is Priceless
Respect and Love for a Defective Church

Canto 20 — 197
Marketing Hope

Canto 21 — 202
Society Serving the Selfish
Fighting Back Without Diminishing Ourselves
A Culture of "Fine Print"

CONTENTS

CANTO 22   211
The Ultimate Weakness of Evil
The Disintegrating Power of Evil

CANTO 23   219
Evil Is Never Unpunished
The Christian Life Frees Us From Burdens
Joyless "Saints"
Walking With a Clear Conscience

CANTO 24   233
Depending Upon the Opinions of Others
Stumbling Blocks and Stepping Stones
Perseverance on the Long Road
Financial Freedom and Freedom of Conscience

CANTO 25   242
Work as an Extension of Ourselves
Identity Theft

CANTO 26   249
The Solitary Path
Special Gifts and Special Responsibilities
Gifted Failures
Gifts as God's Investments in Us
Demagogues and True Leaders

CANTO 27   261
Words That Punish Us
Holding Our Tongue
Blame and Avoidance of Blame

CANTO 28 — 267
   Refusing to Give In
   Humility and Believing
   Us and Them
   Sacrificing for Unity

CANTO 29 — 278
   Hardness of Heart Is Easy
   Family Bonds and Family Feuds
   The Trust That Binds Together Society
   Lack of Empathy and Lack of Manners

CANTO 30 — 287
   Individuality as God's Gift, Not Our Decision
   Sin as the Ultimate Reality Show

CANTO 31 — 295
   The Power of Silence
   Perspective and Experience in the Spiritual Life
   Natural Gifts and Supernatural Glory

CANTO 32 — 304
   The Gradual Freezing of Love
   The Enduring Power of Hate
   The Pain of Betrayal
   As Good as Our Word

CANTO 33 — 315
   Desensitizing Power of Sin
   Climbing Into Our Own Little Pit

CANTO 34   325
The Overwhelming Emptiness of Evil
The Futility of Rebellion
Self-Inflicted Punishment
The Disappointing Spectacle of Evil
The Inescapable Providence of God
The Imprisoning Burden of Sin

FOREWORD

"That's a horrible place," said one of my students upon leaving class, in a comment hardly above a whisper, after I had introduced them to Dante's Inferno.

"You're right," said her friend. "I sure don't want to go there."

I have sometimes heard modern Catholics try to dismiss Dante as merely "medieval," and as indulging himself too much in the gross delight of seeing sinners punished in peculiar ways. My response to that, as I'd tell my students, is that of course Dante could only use his earthly imagination to try to picture for us what it means for a human soul to be separated from God, his source and end, for all eternity. But the imagination is not up to the task. The reality must be far worse.

Be that as it may, in this candid and uncompromising and yet tender-hearted work, Father Paul Pearson shows that he understands what Dante was all about. He meant to provide us with cautionary and admonitory tales, so that he and we would not fall for the evil that the enemy holds forth for us. The Inferno is not a presumptuous outline of what lies in store for adulterers, loan sharks, con artists, assassins, and traitors. It is a profound analysis of what sin actually does to the human soul. We need not wait for entrance into hell for the punishment to begin. It begins with the sin; in fact, it is the sin, setting its roots down into the soul, deforming it, and draining it of health. Dante never merely shows us that a thing is evil. He shows us in scenes of great dramatic power what the evil is and what it does, both to the doer and to the human community.

Father Pearson has written for the benefit of all Christians who want the best and most honest advice on how to advance in the spiritual life, or how simply to stay on the right road of pilgrimage, and not be robbed and beaten bloody by the temptations that would waylay us. At every step his comments are wise and clear. Do not fail in your courage, he says at the outset, suggesting to us what it might feel like, at the end of our lives, to know that we could have accomplished something good or great for the Lord, but did not do so, because we were timid, or lukewarm in our love. Do not be mastered by your passions, he says, again and again, no matter whether they are for physical pleasure (what is sometimes called "love") or for gain (what is sometimes called "ambition") or for the indulgence of wrath (and it is fascinating to see, in our time, that a society exhausted with lust must turn to political hatreds to persuade itself that it is still alive).

But Father Pearson's advice is not mainly negative. Again and again he reminds us that Jesus died for our sins, and that God loves us with a relentless love—if only we would be humble enough to accept that love, to acknowledge that we cannot save ourselves. We are on a journey, all of us, as he astutely says. The details may differ from pilgrim to pilgrim, but the journey is the same, and the Way is the same: "I am the Way, the Truth, and the Life," says the Lord. So it would be foolish in us not to profit from the wisdom of those who have gone before us. Father Pearson sees in Dante the same spiritual advice that you will find in others who have written about the spiritual life, particularly in the founder of his oratory, Saint Philip Neri.

Dante needed the assistance of a guide, Virgil, embodiment of human reason though deprived of the gospel, to make his way down the spiraling circles of hell. Father Pearson is himself a worthy and trusty guide for the reader, whether he is already a lover of Dante, or whether he is green and perhaps even a bit daunted by the prospect of reading an epic poem, as the seminarians at the oratory were. I have been reading and teaching Dante's *Divine Comedy* for thirty years, and so you might think it unlikely that I would come upon a wise interpretation I had not encountered or thought of before, but Father Pearson has provided just that and done so with a grace and ease that is immediately appealing.

A final point. We are coming upon the seven hundredth anniversary of the completion of *The Divine Comedy*, says Father Pearson. A few years ago we lovers of Dante marked the seven hundred and fiftieth anniversary of the poet's birth. Modern man may believe that he has nothing much to learn from the old Florentine. Modern man is a fool if he believes so. He is an incorrigible re-inventor of wheels, moral, cultural, artistic, and theological wheels, but unlike the wheels of old, those of modern man bump clumsily along, because modern man is impatient with the natural law, and will not deign to make his wheels round. Father Pearson sees not only that we can learn much from Dante. He sees that we had better start learning—and that we can have a rousing time of it as well.

PREFACE

The year 2020 marks the seven hundredth anniversary of the completion of Dante's *Divine Comedy*. The anniversary of one of the most important literary works of the Middle Ages would be ample justification for the publication of a new book on Dante, especially for someone trained as a medievalist, but I must admit that I had no conscious intention of writing one.

This book really began not in a library or at a scholarly conference but in a seminary chapel at a spiritual conference more than twenty-five years ago. I was instructing a new crop of seminarians in *Lectio divina*, a method of meditating on a text from Scripture, drawing from it an application to our own individual life and forming particular resolutions for us to follow to put our prayer into effect. It quickly became obvious that prayer was not where this conference needed to begin. The fine points of meditations were not the problem; reading and interpreting the scriptural texts was their main stumbling block. The metaphors and parables of the Gospels might as well have been in a foreign language to some of them. But these young men needed to understand scriptural passages profoundly if they were to pray with them in a way that would transform their own lives and, ultimately, if they were effectively to draw on them to preach to congregations around the world. Something needed to be done.

    I decided to offer a seminar on Dante's *Inferno* in which we would read the text together aloud and interpret it as we went along, passage by passage. The course would function like an apprenticeship in reading spiritual literature, and we would practice together. I intentionally did not tell them that the *Inferno* was epic poetry; that might be more than they would be willing to bear! This approach seemed to make some sense to me since Dante himself had said that he intended to write the *Divine Comedy* in the manner that God revealed Scripture—simultaneously using a variety of levels of meaning. The skills we might develop reading Dante should be transferable to the reading of Scripture. But what would these young men make of a poem from 1320 about hell? They seemed even more distant from Dante's world than a comparison of the dates would suggest, and they certainly were not budding scholars of medieval poetry. Was my own love of the *Divine Comedy* and my training blinding me to what would be productive for these young seminarians? Could they possibly connect with the text?

    Although they were, at first, quite dependent upon my regular interventions to help them make sense of the text, they were almost immediately fascinated by it. What Dante was saying moved them. They might not be fans of poetry, but they had entered seminary because they were interested in pursuing a path toward holiness and helping others to walk that path with them. They found in Dante's text an unexpected source of help for that journey. His text seemed a natural fit for them as they began to focus on their spiritual life with greater dedication. And so the *Inferno* seminar soon became a fixture in the seminary, with the students who had just completed the course encouraging the next year of students to request it. Later, seminars in *Purgatorio* and *Paradiso* were also being offered; once they had begun the journey with Dante, they wanted to continue. I can only hope that the excitement that reading Dante has generated in years of seminarians and the spiritual nourishment they have received as a result of their reading his text will be shared by a wider readership.

The original experience of approaching the *Inferno* with the seminarians also shapes my current text. This book has something of a twofold purpose. It tries to provide a running commentary for a modern reader with primarily spiritual interests who is currently reading the *Inferno*. I hope that the line-by-line commentary will provide serious readers with an experience similar to what the seminarians had in class and will be a help to readers who might otherwise be too intimidated by the *Divine Comedy* to take on the project of reading it on their own.

But there is a second motivation for this book as well. Dante's insights and imagery are so powerful and revealing that anyone interested in the life of the spirit, whether inclined to reading the classics of literature or not, should be immersed in them. For that reason, this book also offers topical headings to guide the reader with a primarily spiritual interest to particular spiritual topics in the text. Someone interested in the evil of violent crime can find Dante's treatment easily. If betrayal of trust is what concerns you, follow the headings to where Dante meets those who betrayed family, friends, or their country. Dante might be a poet writing long ago, but he is a Christian of incredible spiritual and psychological perception. His images etch themselves into the soul. They have the power to change lives.

At the time of the publication of this volume, the Toronto Oratory is in the midst of a capital campaign, *Renovatio*. An important part of the purpose of the campaign is the construction of a new building to accommodate the growing number of seminarians for Saint Philip's Seminary, which is under the direction of the Toronto Oratory. The dormitory space and new classrooms will make possible the training of new generations of seminarians for the Church. For the duration of the campaign, all royalties from this book will be contributed to the building fund.

Perhaps it should not come as a surprise then that this volume is dedicated to the seminarians at Saint Philip's Seminary—past, present, and future. It continues to be an honor to be involved in the formation of good and dedicated priests. I hope that they, who have entered seminary with the intention of becoming saints themselves and leading others on the same path, will follow in the footsteps of Dante in the *Inferno*, whose divine calling it was to guide his readers from the darkness, fear, and confusion of this crazy world of ours "out to see, once more, the stars" (34:139).

ACKNOWLEDGMENTS

Love for the *Divine Comedy* was instilled in me at a relatively early age by the efforts of some very fine teachers. All the way back in high school, we were introduced to large excerpts from the *Inferno* by enterprising young teachers. University and graduate school cemented the connection. At Cornell College, in the Western Civilization program with William Carroll, I was guided through the complete *Comedy* for the first time. Ashley Crandell Amos of the Pontifical Institute of Mediaeval Studies in Toronto encouraged me to investigate fascinating structures in Dante's work in her Vernacular Literature course. She pushed me at the time to publish the findings, but it has taken me well over thirty-five years to take her kind advice. I wish I could have spoken with her about this project. May she rest in peace.

I thank also the members of my community. It has been said that raising a child takes a village, but it is certainly true that forming a seminarian takes a community. In their different ways, they all contribute to the success of the seminary through teaching, spiritual direction, and the myriad tasks that make housing and feeding dozens of people possible. Without their support, I could not have completed this book.

I remember with gratitude the seminarians of Saint Philip's Seminary. They were the original inspiration for teaching a course on the *Inferno*. They have forced me to rethink and clarify my thoughts in a way nothing but a classroom of students can do for me. I could not have written this commentary except as a byproduct of our debates in class and our discussions in my office. Many of them have provided materials about Dante and encouraged me about publishing this text. I hope they understand what an important part they have played in the formation of this text and in the day-to-day happiness of my life.

Throughout the years, I have made use of a great number of wonderful translations of the *Divine Comedy*. Dante's work has drawn the attention of some amazingly talented translators; each one has brought something beautiful and splendid to the wonderful task of reading Dante. It is an exercise in literary wonder to read and compare their attempts to capture the dignity and music of Dante's verse. Dorothy Sayers, John Sinclair, Mark Musa, Allen Mandelbaum, and even the *Naxos* recording of the *Divine Comedy* read aloud have all had a regular place in our classroom. Their renderings of the text and their notes have inspired and guided us along the way. But special thanks must go to Anthony Esolen. Since his translations have appeared, they have been the text of choice for our seminars. His clarity and spiritual sensitivity have been a great gift to us. The references I make within the text to Dante's words are almost always to Esolen's fine translation. Readers could do no better than to

ACKNOWLEDGMENTS

have it open beside them as they make their way through this book, reading Dante's text a little at a time while reading these commentaries along with it.

Knowing my hesitations about writing, God seems to have provided an almost embarrassing crowd of friends to support (and push) me. Several of them have read the text in one version or another. Thank you to my very first readers: Veronica and Bill, Donna, and Danielle, in particular. It took an entire family to get me photographed. The Wyczolkowski family helped me to overcome my discomfort by their friendship and good humor; their work was a complete family effort.

Getting the text ready for publication is a long process. It began in earnest with Fr. Juvenal Merriell providing suggestions and corrections for me. I especially appreciate his keen historical mind and scriptural knowledge. He put me on the right track on many occasions. My own feeling overwhelmed at the idea of presenting a book for publication left me rather paralyzed. The text was relatively complete, but I had done nothing about looking for a publisher. Another Oratorian confrere came to the rescue. Fr. Daniel Utrecht, the author of the very important *The Lion of Münster*, was my literary matchmaker, introducing me to his editor at TAN Books, John Moorehouse. John has been generous and understanding about calming my "first-time" anxieties. He has made the process as painless as possible—at times, it has been very enjoyable!

My final thanks goes to a man named Dante Alighieri. His work is still bearing fruit after seven hundred years. When reading his text, I know I am in the presence of a literary giant but, even more important to me, also an intensely serious Christian soul. Here is a man firmly dedicated to getting his soul to heaven, and to bringing all of us along with him. There is no greater work than that.

INTRODUCTION

A list of great books, classics that every educated person should have read, can seem inspiring at first. We might think to ourselves, *Ah, here is my intellectual project for the next few years, a way of enriching my mind in the privacy and comfort of my own home.* Perhaps we begin at the top of the list chronologically with Homer, or perhaps we look for something we think will be a gentler intellectual "warm-up" for our minds, unaccustomed as they now are (if they ever were) to such exertion. But the list is an impressively and intimidatingly long one. If the size of the list is not enough to discourage one from even beginning, the difficulties presented by a text from a very different culture and distant age can seem daunting. I found it so much easier to attack these great works as a student. Was that merely because I was younger then? Or was it because I had a guide to explain the difficulties and classmates with whom I could discuss my own perceptions while I was compelled to listen to theirs? For many people, the wholesome project of making one's way through the classics is often set aside: not exactly rejected, but put on a sort of permanent hold.

Many people would place Dante's *Divine Comedy* on their list of great books. Dante is someone we really *should* read. He is, by all reports, one of the literary greats the human race has produced, not to mention one of the founding fathers of Italian literature. So why have we not read his greatest work yet? What is it that holds us back?

The reasons a modern reader might hesitate to pick up the *Divine Comedy* are subtle and varied. The first amounts to a sort of intellectual inferiority complex. We absolve ourselves from reading this unquestionably great work by telling ourselves that reading an epic poem written seven hundred years ago about something so dry and dire as hell is obviously something best left to experts. Like many things that we are told are good in themselves, perhaps reading Dante should come with the warning, "Do not try this at home." Specialists in medieval studies, or in literature, or Florentine history, or theology are welcome to slog their way through the text. But it would be wasted on me, so the little voice inside us might say. There is something true in what that little voice says. There is certainly enough in the *Divine Comedy* to keep several different graduate departments of many universities busy indefinitely. For the seven hundredth anniversary of the completion of the *Divine Comedy*, those specialists will undoubtedly be very busy adding to the impressive collection of serious intellectual work already dedicated to Dante. He might have ended his life in exile from his homeland, but he has been treated with enormous respect and veneration by armies of scholars around the world.

But the truth is that Dante did not write his *Divine Comedy* primarily for specialists. He wrote for a much wider audience, an audience as broad as the Church itself. He wrote it for anyone serious about the spiritual life. He wrote it for anyone interested in going to heaven but aware of his own limitations and failings. It *is* a work of amazing complexity, but it is also very direct and immediate, communicating truths from one struggling soul to another. Dante sees himself not only as a literary craftsman, theologian, political philosopher, and crusader for justice, although he is definitely all of those things. More fundamental than those secondary roles, Dante presents himself as a sort of spiritual "Everyman," a pilgrim who represents each one of us on the journey he takes. What he is experiencing on his pilgrimage is something common to us all. His struggles will be familiar to the everyday people for whom he writes. He wants to inspire serious believers to follow him on the road to conversion. Inspiring literary scholars to write articles and books is not enough. He consciously takes up the task of converting hearts and changing lives. If only scholars read his work, he has fallen tragically short of his goal.

Dante at least *hints at* his spiritual mission in the opening line of *Inferno*. "Midway upon the journey of our life..." (1.1). What he is going through is not something peculiar to him; it is part of the human condition. He is not undertaking the journey of his own life only but the journey of *our life*. The lessons he learns are intended for us as well, and the benefits he receives on the way and the promises made to him belong to us too.

But Dante's special mission to lead others on the spiritual path he himself has traveled is more than something we glean from his opening words. Dante reports that it was entrusted to him by none other than Saint Peter himself in his account of his journey through paradise. These are the words Saint Peter spoke to him: "And, seeing the truth about this company, / comfort yourself and others with hope's power, / hope, that on earth stirs love for the true good" (*Paradiso* 25.43–45). Dante is to take his experience of hell, purgatory, and the blessedness of heaven back to earth to kindle in his own heart and the hearts of his readers a desire and hope to share in that blessedness themselves. He has been granted his journey both for his own conversion and salvation but also for his training as a sort of missionary of heavenly hope. Dante intends this book for you; it will not be over your head, but it will challenge your heart.

Many contemporary Christians would hesitate to read the *Inferno* for a second, more theological, reason. The very notion of eternal punishment seems, at first glance, to contradict our image of a loving and merciful God, because, as many modern thinkers like to tell themselves, they have moved well beyond the medieval notion of divine vengeance. In the modern worldview, God's merciful love and the eternal punishments of hell do not seem to be reconcilable. And so, in our society, we hear less and less about even the *possibility* of hell. Even Catholics seem to give an ever-decreasing amount of attention to eschatology—death, judgment, heaven, and hell. We seem to be losing the tradition of praying for the souls of the dead; praying for them implies that there is an uncertainty about their spiritual state after death, an uncertainty that we are not ready to admit. Many people seem to assume that death means immediate entry into heaven. And so, when people die, eulogies are given that celebrate their lives; Masses are celebrated in white that tell us to be confident in the resurrection. We develop an ever-increasing list of euphemisms for death to allow us to avoid even naming the reality. People no longer die; they merely pass. Death is an unwelcome subject. Reading an entire book about eternal judgment might seem unspeakably foreign and distasteful to a contemporary Christian and might call all of these comfortable modern assumptions into question.

But perhaps a questioning of these assumptions is not necessarily a bad thing. What if the societal shifts in focus are not healthy theological developments but rather defense mechanisms for avoiding difficult truths? Our Lord himself, the bringer of the Good News, is the source of most of the references to hell and eternal punishment in Scripture. This is not something later Christians invented. It goes back to Christ himself. He came to us to offer the possibility of salvation, to put before us the choice between life and death. He comes in a spirit of forgiveness so that we can escape an eternity of unhappiness, but only if we are willing to accept that forgiveness and turn away from what separates us from him. Believing in a merciful and loving God does not eliminate the possibility of judgment or of eternal punishment.

God offers us the opportunity for a loving relationship with him—a gift almost impossible to imagine. But a loving relationship is not really a relationship if it is one-sided; it requires a reciprocity of mutual love. There is no question but that *God* desires our salvation. The question is whether *we* desire it. It would be horrible to imagine a universe created by a God who cared nothing for us, but it is horribly sad to consider a world in which God's creatures seem to care so little for him, or for themselves. We seem willing to jeopardize our relationship with him for a passing pleasure. We seem willing to gamble our own happiness on things which we know, at least deep down, will not satisfy.

Dante clearly believes in God's merciful love. In his understanding, eternal punishment is not something imposed by God, as though he were spending all eternity hurling pain and vengeance upon unfortunate souls. Dante's depiction of hell is surprisingly free of the stock pictures of punishment being inflicted. There are almost no devils with pitchforks in the *Inferno*. When they do appear, they provide a sort of comic relief. The horrible sadness of hell resides not so much in the various punishments themselves. What really hurts is the fact that they are self-imposed by souls who choose to hold on to their sins rather than accept the wonderful offer of Divine Love. The punishment of hell arises from our rejection of God, not his rejection of us. It is twisted desire that inflicts the pain, not God. He is constantly intervening to encourage us to escape into his merciful arms.

The subject matter itself will provide a third reason for some people to avoid reading the *Inferno*. Reading a book about souls who suffer forever in hell might seem to indicate a morbid fascination with death and eternal punishment, a twisted and tortured psychology. But morbid fascination is certainly not an element of Dante's personality. He was no narrow-minded, scrupulous, religious fanatic. He spent the first part of his life deeply involved in politics (which earned him exile) and writing love poetry! He is a man of great personal balance and shockingly clear psychological insights that most modern readers would never expect from a "medieval" author.

Dante does not write *Inferno* so that his readers can indulge in a voyeuristic tour in which the reader is invited to stare at *those sinners* down there with their horrible (but definitely inventive) sufferings. In his narrative, there is nothing of the smug self-congratulation that we often associate with the morally doctrinaire. Dante writes for a much more hopeful reason. He is convinced that the sufferings of hell are really just a distillation or permanent snapshot of the natural byproducts of sin, side effects we already begin to experience here in this life. What we see *there* is a revelation of the true nature of sin, once its alluring disguise is stripped away. As a result, *Inferno* is not merely about *them*; it is about *us*. And it is not only about the way we might be some day; it reveals the way we are right now. Dante's descriptions of the torments of hell are a spiritual and psychological reflection on the twistedness of sin, a twistedness that causes us to suffer terribly, but often in an unexpected and hidden way. These sufferings might seem to arise from nowhere or from the very fabric of human existence, making our life seem desperate and the search for happiness futile. If suffering is somehow built right into life, then we can hope for nothing better than what we already have. This messed-up world is as good as it gets. We are left with human life that seems to correspond with Thomas Hobbes's famously distressing formulation: "solitary, poor, nasty, brutish, and short."

Identifying a *cause* of the suffering that is so obvious in our world, as Dante attempts to do here, is not morbid; it is hopeful. Once the source of the pain is located, there exists the hope of a cure. Diagnosis precedes treatment. If the life of sin brings with it the necessary side effect of suffering, then the life of virtue holds out to us the promise of a true and enduring happiness. Dissecting the psychology of sin is part of Dante's message of hope. Life can be different because *we* can be different, if only we choose to get back on the path of virtue.

But all of these justifications for not reading the *Inferno* are based upon a misinterpretation of Dante's intention. The modern reader who steers clear of Dante is doing so most probably because he is missing Dante's point, a point he declares in his choice of title: *Divine Comedy*. Many modern readers will hear the word *comedy* and expect something funny, but the classical understanding of comedy is both broader and deeper. According to the dramatic tradition that dates at least from the ancient Greeks, drama happens in two distinct forms that follow different trajectories. One sort begins with a seemingly idyllic and peaceful scene that appears stable and secure but falls apart because of some hidden flaw or injustice—this is tragedy, the story of the disintegration of human happiness. But there is another sort of drama, one that begins with what appears to be a horribly complicated mess. There is little hope of any resolution of these difficulties. The characters are almost stuck in their situations, with something apparently immovable impeding the possibility of their happiness. But something happens, often an unexpected intervention, that almost miraculously unravels the knots; the happiness that seemed impossible is now a reality—this is comedy.

When Dante chooses to call his poem a comedy, he is

informing his readers of what he thinks can be the trajectory of our lives. We begin in the mess of our fallen human nature, a mess further complicated by our own history of hurts and of personal sins. We get so entangled that we can despair of ever finding our way to freedom. We can find it difficult to *imagine* being free. We are stuck in our mess.

But an intervention happens. In a general way, this assistance from outside is an image of God's grace at work in our souls, most particularly through his entry into our world through the Incarnation. He brings with him new power and new possibilities. But this acting in our world is very particular as well. Each one of us is being showered with graces. Each one of us is being supported by the prayers and good works of the angels and saints. The heavenly kingdom is working together, almost conspiring, for our salvation. With this awareness of the infinite power and support of heaven, we can enter into our spiritual life with an attitude completely transformed. Everything is possible, even our becoming *saints*.

If Dante's poem is truly a comedy, it is less about hell itself than about the wonderful escape that God has planned for each of us. The mess of our lives need not be permanent. We are not doomed to a life without joy. But for the comedy to unfold properly, we need to step enthusiastically into our role. We must accept God's offer of forgiveness and turn away from the disordered attachments that stand in the way of our happiness, both here and forever.

At first, Dante surveyed the ruin of his life—in exile, stripped of his possessions and his reputation—and saw nothing but tragedy. Everything he had, he seemed to have lost. He neither saw the cause of his own bitterness nor had the desire to detach himself from it. It took a heavenly intervention, and a trip through hell, to turn his life around. He writes of his journey in the hope that our paths can be diverted too. He invites us to come with him on his journey, to look at the ugly cause of human bitterness and to discover the way out of our pain. He is recalling the crisis every soul must encounter. He wants us to know there is a way out of the "dark wilderness" in which we find ourselves. We too can discover the comedy scripted for us from all eternity. Welcome to the journey.

> Paul Pearson of the Oratory
> Toronto
> Feast of Our Lady of the Most Holy Rosary
> 7 October 2018

THE INFERNO

CANTO 1

Wandering From the Path
Self-Sabotage in the Spiritual Life
Rejecting Our False Self-Reliance
Learning to Hate Sin

Nothing can expose our vulnerability more vividly than the experience of being lost. Perhaps we have been hiking confidently through the wilderness, secure in our sense of direction, enjoying the splendid scenery, and basking in the beauty of creation. Life is good. A moment comes, however, when an expected landmark is not where we calculated it would be. Nothing seems to indicate the right path. Perhaps we dash around trying to find the path, but our growing sense of panic only makes matters feel more desperate. And since none of our friends or family knows where we are hiking, no one will know where to begin to look for us. We are on our own. The world that moments ago seemed so beautiful and comforting now seems threatening, as though conspiring against us and tracking us down, like a predator out to get us. We are alone and afraid. How did we manage to get off the path? How could we have been so careless? It is our own fault; we know that. But this realization only makes the feeling worse. But this wandering takes on an eternal importance when we have lost the path in our journey to God.

1   "Our life . . ." The opening line draws us into the narrative. Dante intends his account of his own personal struggle against sin to be more than autobiography; it is intended as a sort of parable of the human condition. Although much of what Dante says is highly personal in nature, almost confessional, we are meant to take the journey with him, to learn the lessons that can apply to our own lives. St. Philip Neri would agree wholeheartedly. He had a maxim that his followers recorded after his death: "He who does not go down into hell while he is alive, runs a great risk of going there after he is dead" (15 November). Welcome to that spiritual journey! Enter into it with eyes and ears open, and, even more importantly, with hearts open. This is *for you*, and, in a real sense, this is *about you*.

4   We often bluster when we are lost, confused, or bewildered. We pretend to know where we are and where we are going, we pretend to be courageous, but we *know*, in our heart of hearts, that we are indulging in make-believe, whistling in the graveyard. Dante's reaction to being lost, however, is very straightforward and

honest: he is afraid, so afraid that he can hardly bear to remember it.

We might avoid admitting it, but life often brings this sort of fear out in us, especially when we seem to have lost our way. We cover it up as a lack of confidence, or a bad self-concept, but the truth of the matter is that we, too, are afraid. Dante wants us to face the fears we encounter in our lives without the need to retreat to playacting. The "dark wilderness" of our lives (we all have it) *is* frightening. Let's not pretend. This *fear* is really the theme of the first couple of cantos of the *Inferno*.

10 We might know when we *discover* ourselves to be lost, but just exactly when we *became* lost is unclear. How we get lost is often difficult to pinpoint because it is the culmination of thousands of little choices, the product of lukewarmness more often than determined evil. There usually isn't a dramatic moment when we choose decisively to leave the path. We wander more than choose. A little off the path here, a little more there. When did we stop saying those prayers that were once so regular a part of our life? When did that bad habit really become a habit? It is a death by a thousand cuts.

Perhaps that is why Dante's recognition that he is lost happens only "midway upon the journey of our life." It takes a while to get ourselves thoroughly off track. The modern world would refer to this as a sort of "mid-life crisis," a product of innumerable choices that land us in a place we had no intention of entering. We are bewildered: how did we get here? How did it come to this? What happened?

Dante describes himself at the time of his wandering as "so full of sleep." Perhaps he is referring to the way passion can lead our intellects into a sort of moral slumber, dulling our conscience so that we barely notice when we leave the path. We become so accustomed to the wrongs we do, so weary of fighting, that we come to a place where we really stop noticing that what we are doing is in fact wrong. Conscience has been lulled by the lullaby of the world and our bodily desires, until finally its eyes begin to close.

16 We see in a dramatic way the stages we pass through once we recognize that we have lost the way. First, we are afraid and bewildered. Second, and this is where Dante is at the moment, we are convinced that we can cope. Dante experiences hope at the rising of the sun, which he sees as a glimmer of light over the hilltops. He thinks he sees the way out of the dark woods, out of the problems into which his life has descended. How often men talk themselves into thinking that they can solve their problems on their own—never ask for directions! Like Dante, we tell ourselves that we can calm down: it will all be fine. We know just what we need to do to get back on the right path. Misplaced confidence fills our hearts like a reveler making New Year's resolutions while filled with champagne. We mean them when we say them, and saying them gives us a warm glow inside. How many of our bold resolutions come to nothing almost immediately? Think of the alcoholic swearing off the drink, or the adulterer who says he'll never be unfaithful to his wife again. They might mean what they say, but what would you predict about their future?

> WHEN we recognize that things are going badly and we are wandering off the path, why is it so difficult for us to get back on it? Unfortunately, the answer to that question is not some external force or obstacle; it is something self-generated that arises from within us. In the spiritual life, we are often our own worst enemies. Our good resolutions and carefully designed plans often fail as a result of an act of self-sabotage. The beasts inside us keep us from doing what we so devoutly planned. Saint Paul called it the "old man." But whatever we call it, we know it lurks inside of us, thwarting our good intentions.

31 Dante's confidence is short-lived. Just "where the steeper rise began," just when he faces a challenge that will make a real demand on him, he is stopped in his tracks. When Dante begins his ascent up the hill, towards the light, a leopard blocks his way. His best intentions and desires are thwarted by the beast that is a symbol of the vice of lust.

Here we see one of Dante's important literary devices: his struggles with particular beasts here and his trials in certain circles of hell and terraces of purgatory are a sort of personal revelation. He struggles with those beasts and in those places dedicated to the sins that infect him. Some circles he will breeze through because those sins did not weigh upon his conscience. As a result, Dante's journey is almost like a very personal examination of conscience, exposing to us the weaknesses in his soul that stand between him and true holiness. The first of these impediments is lust, embodied in the leopard that prevents him from making any progress up the hill.

34 No matter how Dante tries to go around the leopard, he can't. The leopard stalks him, "check[s] me in the path I trod." Don't our weaknesses and temptations

seem to attack us at the worst possible time? It is easy to feel like prey being stalked by the predator. Getting away from our habitual sins isn't as easy as it sounds. Those who do not suffer from the habit do not really understand. The habit can leave us feeling helpless, like a small animal held at bay by a crafty hunter.

44 Dante's personal sins are blocking his spiritual progress. Any hope he had of escaping the leopard is dashed when a lion enters the scene as well. The lion is a symbol of pride and perhaps also of the anger that stems from pride. The lion is "hot with wrath" and is coming straight for him. As an exile, Dante is filled with resentment and rage at what he perceives to be grave injustices inflicted by his political foes. We'll see many instances of Dante's struggles with these faults.

49 The third beast to block Dante's progress is the she-wolf, emaciated, driven by hunger, both personal and on behalf of her offspring, to do whatever it takes to get her prey. She seems a symbol of greed or avarice, "stuffed with all men's cravings." Again, as an exile, Dante would be particularly troubled by the loss of the material goods he left behind and by the desire to reestablish his former standard of living.

> THINKING that we can manage on our own, thinking that it is our duty to manage on our own, is an enormous stumbling block in the spiritual life. The path we are trying to follow is supernatural, beyond our abilities. It is

foolish pride to insist that we can do it ourselves. Most spiritual writers recognize that a transformation happens in us the moment we realize that we cannot trust our own powers, no matter how painful that experience might be. For some people, especially those who do not acknowledge God, self-distrust can lead to a feeling of despair; we have tried everything, we have done everything in our power, and it has not worked. We have nowhere else to turn. But for the believer, learning to distrust ourselves can open us up to trusting the power of God. We will never learn to receive from him the grace we need so long as we are obsessed with strategizing and coping. But what an uncomfortable bit of self-knowledge it is to see that we cannot depend upon our own powers! This is a sort of knowledge that we must almost always acquire by the painful experience of trying and failing, and trying and failing yet again. It is something we see only when we are face-first in the dirt. We discover that we need help, and that is profoundly humbling.

52 Dante's self-confidence has turned to despair. It is the she-wolf, finally, who so weighs Dante's spirit down that he gives up hope of reaching the hilltop. Like a gambler who, knowing when to cut his losses, leaves the table, Dante gives up hope and turns back into the dark valley from which he had struggled to escape. This turning back is not necessarily a bad thing. If Dante, recognizing that he cannot make progress on his own, gives up the spiritual journey, that is a

disaster, a tragedy. If his self-knowledge leads him to ask for and depend upon God's strength, this apparent defeat is the first signal of victory. Before we truly trust God, we must have a sincere distrust of our own powers, a distrust founded upon our direct experience of failure. It is a painful lesson to learn, but that does not make it any less necessary.

65   Dante sees someone and desperately cries out for help. He does not know who it is and does not really care. He wants someone, anyone. "Mercy upon me, mercy! . . . whatever you are, a shade, or man in truth!" His cry is an admission of his own inability to climb the hill and escape the dark wilderness. The person he sees turns out to be Virgil, Dante's role model as a poet, come back from the dead. Virgil only gradually reveals himself to Dante, one clue at a time.

76   Virgil knows perfectly well why Dante turns back and does not climb the hill—that's why Virgil's been sent. He asks Dante so that he'll be forced to put it into words, to admit out loud his helplessness, in much the same way that we must put our sins into words in the sacrament of confession, even though God knows perfectly well what we have done before we tell him. Saying the words, admitting it to ourselves and to someone else, really does matter.

79   The fact that Dante's guide is Virgil is both a blessing and a curse. Obviously, Virgil is someone Dante can trust unreservedly. But, at the same time, being on this

CANTO 1

path with Virgil requires that Dante reveal his failings to the very man he respects most. Dante is forced to humble himself before his hero, the very person with whom he would most want to make a good impression. It is not surprising that his "forehead [was] full of shame."

88 Dante is honest with Virgil and indicates the beast that made him turn away from his ascent. He humbly asks for help: "Save me from her." There comes a time when we get so caught up in sinful habits that we don't have the ability to help ourselves, when the help has to come from the outside, like someone so sick that he can't get the medicine that will cure him.

> WHAT motivates us to accept the help offered to us and to fight to get back on the pathway to heaven? Often pious thoughts about obeying God's commandments or contemplating the wonders of heaven are not enough, not nearly enough. The battle is too difficult to be fought with such delicate weapons. We need a more deeply human, more visceral motivation, something that goes as deep as our attachment to sin. What we need to develop is a sort of gut reaction to the destructive power of sin. We need to feel revulsion for what it does to us. For this reaction to become operative in our soul, we need to see sin as it truly is, in all its ugliness.

91 Virgil indicates that Dante can't merely walk up the hill; that just will not work. "It is another journey

you must take . . . if you wish to escape this savage place." Sometimes good strategies and intentions aren't enough. Something more is needed. Being serious about fighting sin, especially habitual sin, requires developing a *hatred* of the sin and its destructive power. We need to strip away the alluring disguise sin wears and reveal the disorder, the ugliness, and the misery it causes. On his journey, Dante will need to see the destructive power of sin face-to-face. Dickens's Ebenezer Scrooge was sent on a similar journey. This up-close and personal encounter with the power of sin to corrupt our humanity is the ultimate reality show.

97 Perhaps surprising for the modern, sex-obsessed, mind, the beast that Virgil identifies as the most vicious is not the lustful leopard but the ravenous wolf. Lust can be very powerful, but avarice has greater lasting power. Rather than being satisfied with what it is able to seize for itself, avarice grows in its appetite: "after feeding hungers all the more." Avarice also has a sort of respectability about it: we tend to admire those who have "done well for themselves." The social respectability of greed is suggested by Virgil's comment that "many a living soul takes her to wife."

112 Virgil tells Dante that it is best for Dante to follow him "where you will hear the groans of hopeless men." What is it that the trip through hell will give Dante, and through him to us? A very direct and personal knowledge of the *destructive power of sin*. This is the strongest motive in the battle against sin, seeing and, quite reasonably, fearing what it can do to us. This fear of what sin is doing to us (and to those whom we love) can form the foundation of a productive sort of sorrow or contrition for our sins, a sorrow we call attrition. This fear is not just about what *God* will do to us; it is about what continuing on the pathway of sin will do.

Dante is about to learn, and share the lesson with his readers, about just how destructive sin can be. Each soul we meet is an object lesson that should make us afraid of sin with a very healthy sort of fear.

121 Should Dante wish to visit heaven, another guide will have to lead him. Virgil, as we will see, often stands as the voice of reason. Reason can reveal the destructive power and the disorder of sin and the steps necessary (at least some of them) to rid ourselves of that sin. But reason cannot explain the glories of heaven; they are supernatural and require faith. In addition, Virgil isn't welcome there: God, "because I was a rebel to His law, will not allow me entry to His realm." Virgil's own spiritual status and his awareness of it will be a point of ongoing interest.

CANTO 2

Giving Up Hope That We Can Be Different
Isolation in Our Battle

Who are we to think that we can be different from what we presently are? Who are we to think that we are being called to something infinitely greater than ourselves? Given our previous experience of trying to improve ourselves, anyone with any personal honesty would give up before even starting. But still, God seems to call. "What is man that you are mindful of him?" (Ps 8:4). It all seems to be beyond us, a task in which we are bound to fail. And there is something true in that fear; it is beyond our powers. But we are not asked to perform these tasks alone. God's help will be with us each step of the way. When we face our judgment at the end of our life, we will acknowledge all the wrong we have done. But we will also have to admit to all the good we failed to do through fear and cowardice. How much more we could have done, how much more we could have been, if only we had not been afraid, if we had trusted in the power of God's constant help. No matter how overwhelming it might seem, God calls us to holiness, to a life shared with the Blessed Trinity in the splendor of heaven. And all things are possible for God.

10 Dante is concerned with his unworthiness to undertake this journey. It is unclear whether his concern comes from true humility or is merely another manifestation of his fear. When we are afraid, we often make excuses as to why we should not do the thing we fear.

He calls to mind those who, while still alive, have made such journeys before him—Aeneas's journey to the underworld, St. Paul's being taken up into heaven. Who is he to compare with Aeneas, the founder of Rome, or St. Paul, the apostle to the Gentiles? But, even more than this, Dante wants to be reassured by Virgil that what he is about to do is really possible. Is there hope to complete this journey, not merely in the abstract, but for Dante in particular? "If I should enter on this quest, I fear / it would be mad and foolish" (34–35).

This canto, in many ways, is a continuation of Dante's reflection upon the power of fear in our lives and the only effective remedy for that fear: the virtues of courage and hope. It is not enough to believe that heaven is our goal and that forgiveness and purification are required to attain it. That faith is necessary but not sufficient for entering the spiritual journey. If we are to be more than Don Quixotes tilting at windmills and dreaming impossible dreams, we need some reassurance that we, with all our weaknesses and imperfections, can reach the end of the journey. Do we trust that what God is asking of us is truly possible? Will we be provided with whatever is necessary to overcome the obstacles in our way? This hope, as Dante's discussion with Virgil will show, is more than whistling in the dark or the power of positive thinking; it is founded on something real, solid, and intensely personal.

37 Dante describes beautifully the psychology of fear, self-doubt, and second thoughts: "as a man who unwills what he wills, / changing his plan for every little thought, / till he withdraws from any kind of start." When faced with a difficulty, we find that any little consideration can be turned into a reason for giving up. The gears of the mind merely spin without gaining any real traction. We vacillate from one option to another until it seems almost impossible to decide anything at all. We become paralyzed with indecision: "for thinking ate away the enterprise." The reality of the struggle can destroy our fledgling hope in an instant, changing our confidence into indecision.

43 Virgil doesn't let Dante off easily or allow him to save face. He correctly identifies the problem, and a humiliating one it is: cowardice. Like a horse that refuses to make the jump, we let our lack of courage stand in the way of what we know needs to be done. Philosophers speak of the irascible appetite, the power where the

virtue of courage is supposed to dwell. It is the desiring power that fights battles by accepting what is painful or difficult when it is necessary or by turning away from pleasures when they are not truly helpful for us. In our world, this power to fight for what is right tends to be woefully underexercised. It is restless inside, squirming for the chance to do what it was intended to do. Think of the people who get addicted to extreme sports or risky behaviors because of the thrill they feel at those moments. They feel "alive" for a change. Courage is an essential part of who we are as human beings. We cannot be fully happy without courage working in our irascible appetite.

But it often happens that this power, out of weakness or indulgence, lets us down precisely when we need to fight battles or undertake difficult tasks: "it turns him from a glorious enterprise." How many opportunities have been wasted in the life of each of us? We all have worldly opportunities we regret having allowed to pass us by: the sports team for which we never tried out, the traveling we never did, the business enterprise we rejected as too risky. Our lives have been lived under the wet blanket of fear, imprisoning our heroic desires and making them no more than ineffectual daydreams.

And the same is true of our spiritual lives. We often *know* what needs to be done, and we even might have a desire to do it, but fear stands in the way—fear of failing, fear of appearing odd or fanatical, fear of losing out on the pleasure the world has to offer. Perhaps this is what Saint John Paul II had in mind when he repeated so frequently that it became almost a trademark of his: "Be not afraid." Do not turn away from "a glorious enterprise." We are created for something heroic; we are diminished as human beings if some share in that glorious enterprise is lacking in our lives.

49 Virgil does not merely humiliate Dante by rubbing his nose in his cowardice. He puts before his eyes the promise of virtue, the promise of freedom: "That you may slip this worry and go free . . ." Step by step, Virgil takes Dante through the process of growing in courage. First, one must develop an honest recognition of the problem. Second, we must train ourselves to hate what the sins do to us and desire the possibility of life being different. Finally, we must develop hope that what we are considering is really possible for us.

In order to strengthen Dante's hope, Virgil tells Dante the story of how he got involved in Dante's case. This way, Dante will see what strong heavenly support he has. He need not (and cannot) depend solely upon his own strength.

> As our world grows and becomes increasingly urban, it is paradoxical that many people experience a sort of loneliness that would have been foreign to previous generations. Although they seem to have little or no privacy, surrounded as they are by people most of the time, they feel alone, left to struggle through life without support or encouragement. This might seem to be even more

> the case for those who dedicate themselves to a serious spiritual life in this secularized world of ours. Who really looks at life the way we do? We are strangers and sojourners in this world, citizens of another homeland.
> But a soul is never alone, never without assistance. Even when we do not perceive this assistance, it is nonetheless active in our lives. This is at least part of what we mean by the communion of saints. The saints and angels in heaven take an active interest in our lives. They are interceding for us and assisting us in ways that often remain hidden from us until we meet them in heaven. If we could live with an abiding sense of their loving concern, how different our lives would feel? That awareness is part of the amazing resilience of the saints.

52 Virgil dwells in a circle of hell that Dante will visit in canto 4. This circle, at least as envisioned by Dante, is inhabited by a rather surprising collection of souls. Dante calls this circle Limbo, but as will be clearer when we read that canto, especially line 26, Dante's description of Limbo is at least distinct from the Church's traditional teaching.

Virgil is visited there by a soul from heaven. This dialogue between them is filled with the language of chivalry—the knight going on a difficult and dangerous journey for his Lady. She is the one who asks Virgil to use his influence with Dante, whom she fears might be too far gone already, but she speaks not merely on her own authority. She has been sent by Saint Lucy and the Blessed Virgin Mary herself. And they are merely instruments of the divine love.

70 The "love" that makes Beatrice bold to speak with Virgil might be, in part, her love for Dante (although she seems rather detached from him much of the time), but, since she is in heaven, it is more likely the love that she has for God and for the fulfillment of God's

plan. She is there, speaking to Virgil, as an instrument of God's will.

79 Like the good knight, Virgil replies graciously to Beatrice's request: "It would be late, had I obeyed already!" Her will is his command. Is this because of her beauty or because she is God's messenger?

88 Our attention returns to the theme of fear and courage. Virgil is perplexed that someone from heaven would dare to venture into hell, or be allowed to do so. Perhaps this is also a subtle dig at Dante: *Beatrice was not afraid to leave the glory of heaven and come down into hell, so why should he be afraid of leaving behind his wandering on earth to venture into hell?* What we rightly fear are those things that truly do us harm. Beatrice is free from any fear of hell because she is beyond being harmed by it. The suggestion is that what God has done for her, he will do also for Dante. He will be protected each step of the way.

94 Beatrice explains that it is not on her own initiative that she comes, but that she does so at the Blessed Virgin's command. (Note that neither Our Lady's name, nor the name of Our Lord, is mentioned in hell. They are holy names and have no place here with souls who have turned away from the infinite good.) It was the compassion of the Blessed Virgin herself that "broke the rigid sentence from above." Her desire for Dante's spiritual well-being is perhaps surprising for those who imagine that the medieval mind was filled with

extreme notions of divine justice. Dante did not picture that we need to negotiate with God, the Blessed Virgin, and the other saints in order to win them over to our side. They are on our side before *we* are, like the shepherd in search of the lost sheep before the sheep either knows it is lost or wants to be found. She doesn't need to be begged; she is the one who sees the problem and moves the others to act. She is the initiator.

97 St. Lucy is summoned by Our Lady to aid Dante: "Your faithful follower now has need of you; I give him over to your loving care." We suppose that Dante had a special devotion to St. Lucy. We see here that our devotion to the saints is reciprocal; the communion of saints is truly social. They work for our well-being even when we don't ask or even know what to ask.

103 Lucy seems to reprimand Beatrice for not having acted already: "Why do you not come to the aid of him who loved you so that for your sake he left the common crowd?" Beatrice says she responded to Lucy's words immediately, but why did she wait until then? Did she not see what those higher in blessedness did? Or was she not moved by what she saw?

Notice that Beatrice herself makes no mention of a special relationship with Dante, but only of obeying Lucy. Perhaps Dante's intense devotion to Beatrice was not fully returned; she might not even have been fully aware of it. Although Dante was married to Gemma di Manetto Donati, who bore him several children, the love of his life, his literary muse, and his guiding light was Beatrice Portinari. Her death, in 1290, drove Dante to immerse himself in Latin literature: Boethius, Cicero, and most especially, Virgil. This dedication to Beatrice was no sordid love affair, filled with scandal. He met her when they were children, and fell in love with her without having anything that we would call a "relationship" with her. He would perhaps greet her in the streets and admire her from afar. This might be the reason Beatrice was rather slow to respond. Dante's feelings were not reciprocated and perhaps not even known. The tears in her eyes (116) are the only indication of being particularly moved by Dante's plight.

123 The reason for recounting Virgil's summons is to give Dante the encouragement he needs. What is there to fear when you have three such ladies behind you? This awareness has its desired effect: "So did my weary courage surge again, and such sweet boldness rushed into my heart I cried out as a man at last set free." We see here the power of moral support, the power of the communion of saints, the power of hope. This *experience* of divine assistance is the foundation of real hope. We know what God has done for us in the past. It is this awareness that gives us reason to trust that this help will continue to be with us in the future. God has invested so much in us already that to abandon us now would be unthinkable. Think of the Magnificat or Queen Esther's prayer before entering the presence of King Ahasuerus. Both were facing mortal danger

(Our Lady, stoning for adultery if St. Joseph rejected her, and Esther, execution for entering the king's presence without being summoned). Both reviewed the blessings God had already granted to them in order to prepare their souls. "The almighty has done great things for me. . . ." In time of struggle, when we are tempted to despair and fear, we need to do the same thing—be grateful, recognizing how much has already been done on our behalf, without our asking for it or even noticing it.

CANTO 3

This Life Is Our Opportunity to Change
Abdicating Our Responsibility
A Principle-Driven Life
The Fatal Attraction of Sin

Hope is a very delicate virtue. It needs to be nurtured by repeated experience of support and reassurance and can soar when everything in life seems to be going our way. Victories can make us feel invincibly confident, but the disappointments of life can batter and wound this confidence and our hope. But regardless of the struggles that life sends our way, we remain convinced of hope's resilience: in the beautiful words of Alexander Pope, "hope springs eternal." There is always another chance, another day to fight. We cannot be so far gone that God could not still help us.

But all of this changes at the moment of our death. The opportunities for conversion come to end. The second chances are not inexhaustible. Our Lord's parables about judgment coming when we least expect it are reminders of the finality of death. We are given the span of our life to work out our salvation, to turn towards God and learn to follow in his ways. For those who refuse to accept his grace, the opportunities come to an end. There are no more possibilities. Hope is eternally lost. Utter hopelessness is the core element of the horror of hell.

1 "I am the way. . . ." We would first associate these words with Our Lord: he is the way, the truth, and the life. When the apostles want to know how to go to heaven, how to follow where Christ is leading, they ask, "How can we know the way; we don't know where you are going?" Our Lord answers that he himself is the way. Those who reject the one way find a very different one, the one Dante and Virgil stand before: the gates of hell.

4 Hell is clearly a creation of God, a product of the "primal love." How can this place of suffering and sorrow, the realm of eternal punishment, be an act of love? The most straightforward answer is that God loves us enough to respect the inviolability of our decisions. When God decides to create free beings, beings capable of knowing him and loving him, the possibility that those free beings will turn away from him is created at the same moment. That freedom, by which we are created in the image of God, is a risky business, and the stakes are high. The existence of human and angelic freedom requires the existence of hell but also makes possible the promise of heaven. Our freedom

is the foundation of our human dignity, and not even our creator will deny our freedom, even if it takes us from him and from our happiness forever.

9   Canto 2 focused on Dante's struggle with courage and hope. Virgil, by recounting to Dante the heavenly intercession that brought them together, has filled Dante with confidence that his heavenly calling, eternal happiness, is still a real possibility. He can look forward with trust to the future. There might be a frightful struggle ahead, but it is a struggle worth fighting because it can be won.

The gates of hell tell a very different story to those who arrive there. Hope means a looking forward to a good yet unattained but attainable. For those entering hell, there is no good to look forward to. They know and know with certainty that their happiness is not here. They do not have it, and they never will. "Abandon all hope." This is the end of the line for human happiness.

15 The theme of hope and trust continues. "Here you must leave distrust and doubt behind, / here you must put all cowardice to death." Again, Dante is warned about cowardice and reassured by Virgil's touch (19). When we are facing fear, words often are not enough. We need some sort of assurance that we will not have to face our trials alone, without support. Virgil's touch gives Dante precisely that personal promise that he will accompany him through whatever comes their way.

We'll see that Virgil's words are more than just a general encouragement. Anyone passing through those gates would certainly need that. But Virgil's words are also a preparation for what we are about to see. We are entering the circle of the neutrals or the lukewarm, those who sinned particularly by their cowardice in life, failing to take a real stand for good, failing to live up to their responsibilities as human beings. We are made for freedom, made for making choices. These people laid aside that fundamental human dignity. They are not only sinners but they are also somehow less than human.

Dante will often use this literary device of using imagery to introduce a circle of hell before we actually experience it. Here the imagery of cowardice prepares us to meet those souls who were afraid to live life. The imagery prepares our mind to encounter what is to come.

ENTERING an adult world full of expectations and responsibility can come as a very unpleasant shock, so much so, in fact, that many people refuse to enter. Thinking about a career, a family, a mortgage, is more than they bargained for. In the face of the overwhelming demands of real life, they retreat into a sort of perpetual adolescence. People might ask them what they intend to do with their lives, but the question feels like a sort of harassment. They are reminded of how promising their lives once seemed to be. They are told of all they could

> still possibly accomplish. But fearfulness (and perhaps a good admixture of laziness as well) pushes them to opt out of ordinary life. Rather than run the risk of failing or go to the trouble of working and struggling, they cop out, living a directionless life devoid of any sense of purpose or drive. For those who love them, it is a terribly frustrating thing to watch: they are wasting their potential. But we so often choose to act in just such a way in our spiritual life, wishing the demands of life (or of God) would simply disappear. Even most people who identify themselves as Christians seem far advanced on the road to apathy and lukewarmness.

18   The "good of the intellect" which these souls have lost is the ultimate good of an intellectual nature, as spoken of by Aristotle: contemplating the highest good, the cause of all things, for all eternity. In Christian terms, they have lost the beatific vision. Remember that these issues are being explained by the pagan Virgil, who will see them through the eyes of reason rather than faith.

22   The imagery here is primarily auditory rather than visual. The reason is simple: it is dark, darker than any earthly darkness could be. This darkness is the polar opposite of the splendor of heaven, where we shall have no need for lamps or the sun, for the Lord God shall be our light. In heaven, we shall see as we are seen. Here we do not see. Following the pathway of sin means choosing the darkness. We are like a blind

man, stumbling in unfamiliar surroundings, with only his hearing and his touch to guide him. This complete failure of sight must add to Dante's apprehension.

24 Dante is overwhelmed by the moaning and wailing he hears. Perhaps this is merely compassion on his part, but perhaps Dante, suffering from his own lack of courage, identifies with these souls. We'll see that Dante suffers most in those circles of hell in which the sins he struggles with are being punished. Dante's reaction in each new circle of hell tells us much about the state of his soul. He is overwhelmed because he experiences some of the same weakness that damned these souls to their torments. How could that growing awareness not be frightening?

29 Aside from the noise, darkness is the dominant image. The light is gone, the light of reason, which is supposed to guide our actions. Here there is no way to know which way to go. Any way seems pretty much the same as any other. The swirling winds add to this sense of directionlessness, a powerful image of the lives of these souls.

34 The fault punished here is that these "sad souls . . . merited neither praise nor infamy." These are the lukewarm spoken of in Revelation: I wish you were hot or cold; because you are neither hot nor cold, I will spew you out of my mouth. Because of being neither one nor the other, not taking a stand, they are welcomed neither in heaven nor in hell proper. They are

like soldiers who would fight on neither side. After the battle, neither army will take them in.

45   "A few words will do." These people are beneath real attention. Their actions aren't fully human, and so they are undeserving of our pity. They "copped out" on life. It is fitting that they remain unnoticed, unremembered. Dante is careful to mention none of them by name. They remain anonymous, like their nondescript lives.

> HUMAN beings have been granted the power of reason so that they can govern their lives according to principles. Made in God's image, we are intended to be lord of our own actions, applying the truths we know to the decisions we make. We are not brute animals driven by our passions or pulled merely by convenience. But this exalted picture of the human race grows ever dimmer in our society. People's principles seem to change with the seasons or the most recent advertising campaign. Taking a heroic stand as Saint Thomas More did, for example, becomes increasingly incomprehensible in our world. Why would he do such a thing? Did he not know what would happen to him? How quickly our world's recognition of the dignity of unborn children has disappeared from the public sphere. How completely the world has lost, seemingly in a single generation, an appreciation for the importance of the family. Where have our principles gone? What has happened to us? We seem to have become back-seat passengers in life rather than those

> responsible for steering. We are so easily driven by media and spin-doctors. Are we in charge of the direction of our lives or are they?

52   "... a banner fly." These people didn't follow principle in their lives, and so here they are driven blindly by the wind in the dark, chasing after whatever banner passes their way. Perhaps following trends or fashions instead of true principles would be included here. Is the slave of fashion living up to his responsibility as a moral and rational being? But can they even *see* the banner in the dark? Perhaps they don't even have as much true intention to their actions as that. See line 64 below.

55   "I had not thought death had unmade so many." Dante is shocked at the number of those included here, in the largest of the circles of hell (since it is at the top of the pit where the circumference is greatest). Lukewarm souls, it seems, are not rare.

64   "These worthless wretches who had never lived ..." Again, their lack of humanity is emphasized. Here they are driven by the stings of flies and wasps; the principle of movement or activity is again from the outside. They are *being driven* rather than *deciding*. Passivity is a key image here, not being "Lord of your own actions," which is the dignity of every human being. As a result, even their blood and tears don't deserve the respect reserved for signs of human suffering; they are gathered up by "loathsome maggots."

> EVERY sinful habit has a distinctively addictive quality. We sin at first because we find the sin pleasant, but we keep sinning even when we begin to realize the destructive power the sin is exercising in our lives. This is why addicts often need some sort of external intervention to begin to get the help they need. But no matter how well-intentioned the intervention, it is almost always resented by the addict. They feel very strongly that friends and family are not helping. They are misguided; they do not understand. They are standing between us and what we desire, what we need. The man who knows that alcohol is destroying his liver still heads to the bar. He might fear what drink is doing to him and to his family, but his desire is stronger than his fear. This "fatal attraction" to sin is both totally irrational but also distressingly familiar.

73 Notice the contrast between the souls being driven by the winds and the wasps and the crowd Dante sees on the banks of the river. The former are passive, while the souls waiting on the banks are eager. "Let me know of those people, and what law / makes them appear so eager to cross over." They have the internal drive and initiative that is so lacking in the lukewarm. We might expect the souls to be screaming in fear, trying to escape the punishment that lies ahead of them. But that isn't the picture. They seem filled with desire, and that desire seems to be for hell. How can that be? This question is an essential one to figure out if we are

going to understand Dante's view of the punishments of hell. They are driven by desire, arising internally from within the sinner.

78   Acheron, the first of the five classical rivers of the underworld we encounter, follows the geography of hell. It is a ring, running the circumference of this circle of hell. It acts like a moat protecting a castle. We'll see this recurring image of hell as a sort of inversion of a city (a sort of anti-heavenly Jerusalem). Think of a medieval city with outer walls, a moat, inner walls, inner fortifications, and finally a citadel in the center.

79   Dante's relationship with Virgil is still dominated by fear and shame. The correction he receives from Virgil produces a response that is out of proportion. This is precisely what happens when we are dependent upon the opinion others have of us.

82   The boatman Charon is a sort of demonic personification of his job. He isn't a human being; otherwise, he would have his own place in the underworld. He isn't a resident—he just works there.

87   Charon tells us that the punishments of hell aren't only the stereotypical ones we've heard of. Along with hellfire, there is also ice. Here the punishments aren't of only one sort. They are especially designed by justice to "fit the crime." As we'll see, they more than fit the sin; they flow naturally from the sin itself.

88   Many people in hell will notice Dante's special status

as a living body. He stands out. He is heavy; he casts a shadow; he leaves footprints. This is not only a reminder of Dante's bodiliness but a backwards way of suggesting the immateriality of everyone else. Dante's bodiliness is the reason Charon tells him he'll have to take another boat. This one is designed to carry only weightless souls.

94 Virgil, the voice of reason, is usually able to command the forces of evil in hell. He merely makes mention of the power under which he acts. He's on a mission from God. Before that divine mandate, hell falls silent. "Then all at once the goatish jowls fell quiet."

112 These souls, which have already been described as eager, here are "gnashing their teeth with fury for their fate" and are hurling "blasphemy at God and at their parents" and wailing bitterly. Charon even whacks the lingerers with his oar. So which is it? Are they afraid or eager? Here we see in these images the conflict of desire that is built into sin—we desire it and the pleasure that comes with it, even while we hate the consequences of the sin. But knowing all of this, we still choose to sin. Every sinner is a person with a divided heart. "The good I will I do not do; the very thing I hate, that I do." Although they know they are headed to their eternal damnation, the souls are driven by their desire. They want it, and they don't want it.

126 What they fear *is* at the same time the object of their desire. The object of their fascination *is* the instrument of their punishment: "what they fear turns into their desire."

133 The earthquake and the slap of lightning is the means by which the all-too-physical Dante is transported over this outer moat of hell.

CANTO 4

God Is at Work in Our Lives
Spiritual Blindness About Our Own Faults
The Potential Goodness of Human Work
Yearning for More Than This World Can Give

We might perceive that we are doing all the work in our spiritual life, that the burden of getting our act together falls entirely upon us, but, in fact, the greater part of the work is being done by God, even while we sleep. As it says in Psalm 127: "Unless the LORD watches over the city, the watchman stays awake in vain. It is in vain that you rise up early and go late to rest, eating the bread of anxious toil; for he gives to his beloved sleep" (v. 1–2).

4   An earthquake and clap of thunder have rendered Dante unconscious. We would expect him to awaken frightened and full of anxiety, but the contrary seems to be true. Dante's "rested eyes" are an image of the refreshment our souls receive from being acted upon

by the divine power. We see here a metaphor of activity in the spiritual life. While Dante rests, God transports him over the river. Real spiritual progress is made, and it is God who initiates it.

7   Again, sound is the first impression Dante receives. He hears the "roar of endless woe" before he sees anything.

10   Hell appears to the viewer as a bottomless pit. Evil is like that—it is dark and without a true focus. Heaven is light and has God as its center. Hell is dark, and peering into it, we see nothing, nothing at all. True evil is as close to nothingness as a being can get. Here that darkness and emptiness is more than an image: it is a physical reality for Dante. They descend into a "blind world," blind because of the absence of that vision that makes us blessed. Like darkness itself, hell manages to be both immense and still claustrophobic.

> ONE of the great challenges in the spiritual life is our own lack of perspective. We seem to have 20/20 vision when examining the faults of others but curious blind spots about our own. We are often unable to identify the plank in our own eye (cf. Mt 7:5). This is precisely why even experienced spiritual directors need a spiritual director! They might be able to produce helpful books on spiritual subjects or guide many on the pathway to holiness, but the one person about whom they lack an objective point of view is themselves.

17   How frail is Dante's new-found courage? He glances over at Virgil and sees him going pale. If his guide is afraid, what hope is there for Dante? But we'll see that Virgil isn't afraid; he is overcome with compassion. Virgil reacts to the circle in an intensely personal way. For Virgil, this circle is not merely an objective place to be visited and understood, as though he were, for Dante's benefit, doing a philosophical survey of the meaning of hell and all of its parts; this circle is *his* circle, the place to which Virgil has been consigned for all eternity. These people are his people, his fellow sufferers. He tells Dante that his paleness is "pity you have taken to be fear."

Where there is so obviously self-interest, we should be careful not to take the narrator's word as objective truth. Virgil has a stake in this circle. His explanation might very well include much that is more self-justification than detached description.

Virgil's paleness is another example of that literary technique Dante uses very consistently, what we can call *anticipatory imagery*. Even before the narrative turns to a new subject, the imagery is already preparing the reader for what he is about to encounter. Before we even enter into limbo, we know that something is up, something that involves Virgil personally. The imagery has done its work, even before the story has begun to be told.

26   Here, in Limbo, the atmosphere of hell changes dramatically. Sound is what Dante first notices, and that

sound is noticeably different: there is no wailing and crying out here but merely sighs arising from "sorrow, without punishment." Here, too, there are children (infants). Dante, as will become clearer, has blended together three different ideas of limbo—one a dogma, one a common theological opinion, and another of Dante's own invention.

The **first** is the *limbus patrum* (limbo of the fathers), the bosom of Abraham, that place of waiting to which the faithful ones before Christ's coming were consigned until his saving death. Because the price for their sins had not yet been paid, these faithful souls had to await Christ's saving death. After his death and before the resurrection, Our Lord descends to the underworld, the "bosom of Abraham," "to free the just who had gone before him."[1] Once Christ descended to them, this place of waiting no longer had a function. If it is still a place, it would be an empty place.

The **second** idea of limbo that Dante incorporates here is the *limbus infantium* (limbo of children), the limbo which some theologians had speculated was the fate of unbaptized babies. This was never an official dogma of the Church but was a common opinion of respected theologians. Recently, high-ranking people in the Church (including Pope Benedict XVI) have called this notion of limbo into question, saying that we can only entrust the souls of unbaptized babies into the merciful hands of God, a hopeful place to be. "As

---

[1] *Catechism of the Catholic Church* (CCC) 633.

regards *children who have died without Baptism*, the Church can only entrust them to the mercy of God, as she does in her funeral rites for them. Indeed, the great mercy of God who desires that all men should be saved, and Jesus' tenderness toward children . . . allow us to hope that there is a way of salvation for children who have died without Baptism."[2]

The **third** idea of limbo is the limbo of the virtuous pagans, a place for those who lived lives of virtue, but only natural virtue. This aspect of limbo is Dante's own contribution, so we must be careful in how we interpret the narrative about it. Our only explanation for it comes from Virgil, and he is not necessarily an objective witness. The reader must listen critically to his words about limbo.

31 Here, unlike elsewhere, it is Virgil who takes the initiative: "You don't ask . . ." Virgil seems to be eager for the chance to explain his own place for eternity, to give an *apologia* for his own life. But is Virgil, who otherwise serves as the voice of reason, truly objective when he describes his own eternal fate? Commentators often seem to take Virgil's words as "gospel" truth, to view him in the role of the "omniscient narrator," but Dante's writing seems to send subtle images and signals that provide contradictory messages. Be on the lookout for these signals; you won't have to wait for long.

---

[2] CCC 1261.

34 "They did not sin." Virgil seems to be saying that the souls in limbo are there only because of a sort of personal bad luck, having been born at the wrong time. They had merits, but these weren't enough without baptism. And for this "falling short, and for no crime," these souls are sentenced to eternity in limbo. It is tempting to be sympathetic; Virgil is very persuasive.

But balanced against Virgil's words is a very basic fact of geography that could easily go unnoticed: according to Dante's description of limbo, they are *in hell*, the first circle of hell to be precise, not outside like the neutrals, but on the "wrong" side of the river. In addition, Virgil, when he first met Dante in canto 1 (line 125), described himself as a rebel against God's law. Here in canto 4 he says, "They did not give God homage as they ought" (38). Isn't that a fault or a sin even for the soul without grace? Honoring God is part of the natural law (this honor is a debt of gratitude to the being who made both you and the universe in which you dwell), which any human being is obliged to obey, even though baptism wasn't available to him. So are these pagans innocent victims or rebels? What sort of merit could they have if they did not have grace?

49 "Has anyone ever left here?" Here again, Dante suggests that Virgil's description of the reason these souls are in limbo isn't what it seems to be. There have been many souls who were here, *unbaptized souls*, who were released at Christ's descent to the dead. These souls were saved without the actual sacrament of Baptism;

they made it to heaven even though they were born before the time of Christ. God must have provided a way for them to be saved. Since he wills the salvation of all, salvation must be somehow possible for all. We cannot say that God wills what is impossible. If there was no way for Virgil and his fellow pagans to be saved, would the fault for that belong to God because he refused to will to make it possible? There must be some reason other than just the lack of baptism for Virgil's being here.

51 Does Virgil sense Dante's suspicion? "He heard the meaning mantled by my words." Dante's gentle reminder of Christ's descent to the dead and the release of the holy souls from the bosom of Abraham leads Virgil to give his own account of the event. It is as though the truth is slowly being pulled from him. Who is guiding whom here? There is a long list of souls who were delivered. We are told merely that "he made them blessed." So the accident of being born before Christ is not an impediment to heaven after all.

63 The gates of heaven were not open until the paschal mystery was complete. This is why the souls of the righteous had to wait for Christ. Their salvation was based on a spiritual sort of IOU; atonement needed to be made for their sins. That atonement was made by the passion and death of Christ. He makes good those IOUs with his saving death. The price had to be paid; justice requires it.

CANTO 4 57

> THERE is no denying the great value of human accomplishments. We are made in the image of God, and every act of the intellect that contributes to the building up of his world is a light that shines in the darkness. The Church bestows its blessings upon human endeavors. We ask for God's blessings upon human labor (in which Our Lord himself participated in the Holy Family), upon the arts that we hope will raise the spirits of those who witness them, and upon those who govern society that they may foster the peace. Every human act, done in accordance with reason, is spiritually precious—a preparation and foundation for the building up of God's supernatural kingdom.

68   "A ring of light / quelling the darkness that surrounded it." Here we see, in a visible way, the splendor of the light of reason, glowing even here in hell, the only place in hell where the light overcomes the natural darkness of the pit. Elsewhere in hell, there will be other flames burning, in fact, plenty of flames burning, but none that really illuminates the surroundings. These hellish flames burn without providing real light. Here, in this illuminated bubble, we'll find souls who were preeminent in human learning in all its branches. Their light, even though it was merely a natural light, shone on their lives and the lives of those around them.

80   Virgil is given a special status here, special even in that circle of the great poets of the classical world. This isn't just an expression of Dante's hero-worship. Virgil is

seen both as a witness to the classical world and reason but also as a sort of prophet of the coming messiah. His poetry (the *Eclogues*) had been seen by many to foreshadow the virgin birth. He is a sort of bridge between reason and faith, almost a pagan prophet.

93 There is no false modesty in Virgil: "They do me honor—and in this do well." He recognizes the gifts he has been given and is not surprised when others recognize them as well.

102 Virgil is part of a very elite group of poets (83). Dante is now included as a worthy member, a sixth in their band. Here he is included, along with Virgil, in the company of Homer, Horace, Ovid, and Lucan. Perhaps not the most modest of things for Dante himself to write, but it shows that Dante sees himself as a true successor to the classical poets, a real Renaissance man, and mirrors the same recognition of gifts that Virgil had. To pretend that we have not received great gifts, when we in fact have, seems ungrateful. Even Our Lady, that picture of humility, acknowledges that the "almighty has done great things for me."

106 Again the image of a castle. This castle seems to be the home of true reason, fully lived humanity, at least in its natural state. Note that there are seven walls and seven gates. I think both of these represent the same reality—the seven liberal arts, comprised of the trivium (grammar, logic, and rhetoric) and the quadrivium (arithmetic, geometry, astronomy, and music).

This learning serves both as a defense of humanity against attack from what is less than fully human (the walls) as well as a means of entering into the true core of that humanity (the gates).

109   The poets seem to walk on water: "Over this stream we passed as on dry land." The power of their reason grants them a regal dominion over the material world. The green field shows the fertility of human thought and contrasts strongly with the desolate landscape in the rest of hell.

114   "Seldom they spoke, and held their voices low." True wisdom is deliberate, slow to speak. It doesn't push itself forward. Wisdom doesn't have a marketing department. Silence is an important part of, and an important preparation for, the wisdom that is praised here. Silence helps to make them wise, and wisdom helps to keep them silent.

> WITHOUT taking anything away from the splendor of human reason and its accomplishments, we are still reminded in countless little ways that human beings are created for something even more dignified. Saint Augustine felt that yearning for God, a yearning that arises from the fact that we are created by God and for God. And because of the way we are created, our hearts cannot rest except in their Creator.

120   Dante exclaims, "Glory it is, to see what I have seen!" There is no denying the "glory" of reason in its natural state. Dante's description of it literally glows. He feels honored to walk in the presence of the greatest poets in history. But we notice that something is missing, some spark we expect among such noble souls and do not

see: even in the souls of these four great poets, there was "neither joy nor sadness in their eyes" (cf. 84).

131 At the center of a sort of "who's who" of the classical world stands the "master of all those who know," Aristotle, who possesses the greatest epithet I can imagine, at least in the natural realm. Closest to him are Plato and Socrates, then other Greek thinkers.

143 Perhaps because of their association with Aristotle, the Arabic philosophers Avicenna and Averroes are included here, even though they are clearly after the coming of Christ. Their inclusion here seems to point to a broader idea of "pagan," encompassing those who didn't have the Christian faith, the fullness of the faith, but who followed the precepts of reason faithfully. Why are they included here while other followers of Islam find themselves with the schismatics? Dante seems to consider these Arabic philosophers more Aristotelian than Muslim, a judgment in which certainly many of their contemporary Muslim theologians would concur, especially in the case of Averroes, who was condemned by them for his stand on the independence of reason from faith.

151 Leaving limbo, we enter into "a place where nothing ever shines," in contrast with the ring of light we found in limbo. Here in hell, each particular sin, each in its own distinctive way, obscures the light of reason. We'll be brought back to this way of thinking of sin over and over again in *Inferno*. Sin is not merely an offense

against God and his commandments but against our own reason and our humanity. This is also why Virgil is a fitting guide to hell. Not only is he a resident, but also he stands for reason, and reason is precisely what sin destroys. What better person could there be then to present that destruction for us?

CANTO 5

Some Sins Are More Destructive Than Others
The Power of Passion
The Human Tendency to Self-Deception
Our Weakness in the Face of Temptation

Which sins we consider the most heinous seem to shift over time and across different societies, sometimes shockingly so. But, despite the theorizing of some theologians, we always appear to have a hierarchy. Sometimes that hierarchy is organized according to the shame that the sinful actions bring on or the scandal they cause. Recently the damage done to others has been the most important consideration. In the Middle Ages, the most important victim to take into account when weighing the gravity of a sin was, perhaps surprisingly, the sinner himself. Every sin could be analyzed according to how destructive it was of the sinner's own humanity. Is the rot something superficial or is the sinner rotten to the core?

2 The circles become progressively smaller as we descend into hell. This is more than just a matter of geometry—more people are present on the upper terraces. The lesser sins are the more common ones.

4 In place of the image of a recording angel at Saint Peter's gate, here, at the gate of hell, we are presented with a judge of a very different sort. Minos is barely human, if human at all. He grunts like a bull rather than speaking. After hearing the sins—which he seems to take delight in: "the sin-connoisseur" (line 9), in Esolen's lovely translation—he wraps his tail around the sinner the number of times that corresponds with the number of levels the sinner must descend in hell. His tail seems to work as a beastly elevator, not merely marking the place the sinner belongs, but delivering the soul there.

Emphasis here is on the dehumanizing effect of sin. Notice how much of the imagery (especially in the regions dealing with sins of passion) is beastly. Before we actually begin to talk about this beastliness of uncontrolled passion, the imagery has prepared us for the idea. We have entered a realm where unbridled passion rules.

14 The souls here testify against themselves. We shall experience the general readiness of the souls here to talk about their sins with Dante. They seem to have no shame, only the desire for their stories to be heard and remembered.

19   "Watch how you enter and in whom you trust!" Again, the imagery reminds us of the importance of trust and hope in the spiritual life. Hell is not only a place in which hope for our ultimate destiny is lost permanently but also a place governed by deceit and lies. Satan, after all, is the Prince of Lies. We should be careful in accepting the statements made by the damned. They are so caught up in their sins that they often cannot help but justify them.

20   Minos's words are a frightening warning, reminiscent of Our Lord's own words: "Don't be fooled by the broad and easy gate." The way into hell is easy; you might even say that it's all downhill from here. But that wide opening is really only one-directional. Hell is easier to get into than it is to get out of!

> It certainly feels as though our passions drive us at times. Their power seems almost overwhelming and irresistible. But even though our passions are an essential aspect of our human nature (we cannot be human without them, regardless of what the Stoics argue), it is also part of our nature as rational beings that our passions should operate in us under the direction of our reason, like horses guided by the driver of a carriage. In their proper place, passions give our actions power and drive—or "horsepower." But if they are allowed to run on their own without proper direction, our actions become little different from those of brute animals. To allow our passions to rule is to abdicate our responsibility as human beings.

21   Virgil silences another beast of hell by referring to the power of heaven. He doesn't request but commands: "No questions." If we take him here as the personification of reason, he shows us the proper relationship between reason and the passions: the rational powers command and the passions are intended to obey. This is the way our human nature is supposed to be ordered.

It is, however, so different from the way we act most of the time that it seems impossible even to imagine. This apparent impossibility is only the result of original sin not the nature of the passions. This ordering of the passions is the goal towards which virtue brings us. The virtues train the powers of the soul, including the passions, to be conformed to reason.

25 Once Minos is quieted by Virgil's command, Dante can hear "wails of sorrow" like a wave pounding the shore. The sense of hearing once again takes the lead, because we are back in darkness, "a place where all light is struck dumb." The light, in particular the light of reason, has been overcome by passion. Like Dante wandering in the dark wood, souls given to their passions are "a people that in darkness dwelt."

31 The souls here are driven by a driving wind, a "hellish cyclone" that "whisks them about and beats and buffets them." As with the neutrals, the imagery is one of passivity, of being driven by forces outside of oneself rather than by the reason God has given us as our guide. Like the neutrals, those who have given control of their lives over to their passions are leading a less than human existence.

But although the imagery seems the same, there is an important difference: this force driving these souls in their sin is interior—their own passions and desires. It might be inspired or moved by something outside of them, but it is pushing from the inside. The neutrals were the weak victims of exterior influences. The passionate are weak but succumb to an influence that is their own desire.

36   Again, curses are directed to God, as though he were responsible for their sufferings. These seem to occur especially when they pass "the ruined slope." This slope was caused by the earthquake at the time of Christ's death and during the harrowing of hell, when Jesus descended to the dead after his crucifixion to deliver the souls of the just from their waiting place: the *limbus patrum* or Bosom of Abraham. These faithful souls could not enter heaven until the price was paid for their sins. This atonement happened when Christ offered himself on the cross for us. Now he has come to announce to them that their time of waiting is over. His dramatic entry to deliver these souls and the resulting damage from the earthquake, as we shall see repeatedly, gives Dante and Virgil their pathway into many of the circles of hell. So perhaps the cursing of these damned souls happens because this is where they entered their circle of hell. It reminds them of their fate. Perhaps it is also a reminder of God himself, whom they have abandoned by their sins and whom yet they blame for their predicament. The ruin is a reminder of the power of *real* love, the love that allowed Our Lord to lay down his life for his friends.

39   Here the lustful are punished "who made their reason subject to desire." This is obviously true of the

lustful, but is also true of all sins of passion. As they were driven by their lust in this life, so now they are driven by the wind that flings them this way and that, without any hope of release or rest.

The image of the starlings driven by the wind is particularly interesting. The wind provides the force, but the wind only drives them because they themselves have spread their wings. Birds have the instinct to stay put in a windstorm. Their wings are tucked in; they are hidden away somewhere safe. This reminds us that one of the important techniques for avoiding sins of the flesh is not putting ourselves into occasions of sin. Spread your wings in a windstorm and what do you expect? Of course you will end up being "carried away."

> POLITICIANS have recently depended increasingly upon "spin doctors," people who can take an event and sell it to the public in a very different way from what we would expect. The passions seem to have learned this strategy long ago. By painting our passions in a noble and appealing way, giving in to them seems natural and fitting, almost glamorous. We might know in our minds that there is a real difference between love and simple sexual desire, but we would be hard-pressed to find that distinction clearly presented in worldly accounts. But this "spinning" happens inside our consciences as well, telling ourselves the most outrageous tales. We appear to fall for those stories on a regular basis. Self-deception is a uniquely human art form.

52 At Dante's request, Virgil identifies some of the souls punished there, including a great number of very famous "lovers." But "lover" is in fact an inappropriate name for them. After all, they're not in hell for loving, but for lust, which is a very different thing. Dante does not seem to keep this distinction clearly in his mind. Perhaps we should not be surprised that someone who spent years writing love poetry might be carried away by such stories of "love."

56 Semiramis, queen of Assyria, altered "lust" to "just" by rewriting laws to allow her to marry her own son. This introduction to the circle of the lustful is a clear example of the way passion leads us to set aside even the clear dictates of reason and strong sexual taboos.

61 Dido committed suicide, but she is punished here. Dante must be presenting the idea that her true sin was lust. Having given herself over to that, she was so overwhelmed by the passion that she was not fully culpable for her suicide.

69 Virgil doesn't hesitate to point out the seedy side of these characters and their lives. Dante doesn't seem to pick up on Virgil's tone but looks on their fate with more sympathy than judgment and thinks of the souls as those "whom love had severed from our life on earth." When Dante speaks, it is of "love" not "lust." Is he still under the spell of the leopard who stalked him in the dark woods? He seems more a fellow sufferer than an objective observer of divine justice at work.

Note his own reference to his sympathetic reaction: "A whelm of pity left me at a loss" (72).

80   God seems to permit Paolo and Francesca to leave off their punishment to speak with Dante. It is important that he learn the lessons necessary for his salvation, and they have something essential to teach him.

82   The two "lovebirds" are eager to grant Dante's request to come and tell him their story. Called in the name of their love ("beg them by the love that drives them on"), they are necessitated in coming to Dante. They are truly slaves of their passions.

The souls in hell are, for the most part, very pleased to speak about why they are there. They want to be heard (today, they'd be on a talk show, baring all). Reader beware, however, as in the case of Virgil's description of why souls are sent to limbo; the accounts these sinners offer often contain much self-justification and perhaps a good dose of self-deception. After all, the first effect of sin in the Garden of Eden was for Adam and Eve to attempt to "cover up" both literally and figuratively.

95   By God's will, talking seems to give some sort of respite from the punishments they endure—"as long as the wind falls in silence."

103 Francesca sees herself as a sort of "victim" of love: "Love that allows no loved one not to love, seized me." She did not *decide*: she was seized, captured by

something far beyond her strength. She uses the same verb to describe Paolo's role.

As she talks, a very romantic tale is told, eliciting sympathy from most listeners. She displays no recognition of the disorder of her appetites, no contrition for the sin committed, no repentance for the harm she did her husband. Notice that she doesn't even really mention at first that the man who killed them was her husband. He is merely "the man who quenched us of our lives." She is first a victim of the love that seized her, and then a victim of the husband who killed her. The extent of her self-absorption is amazing.

113 Dante is moved with pity at the plight of the lovers. His head is bowed almost reverently as he listens. "What great desire, what sweet and tender thoughts / have led these lovers to this woeful pass!" You can almost hear his tone of voice in these words. This tells us something important about Dante. He is compassionate, he feels with them and for them, because he, too, knows the power of the leopard. Dante's own problem with this sin becomes clear in the way he asks his questions: "How did it happen, what made Love give way that you should know the truth of your desires?" It was lust, not love, and it brought them to darkness, not truth. Dante isn't here to share sad stories with unfortunate victims of cruel circumstances. He is here to learn that sin is freely entered into, disordered with respect to reason, and destructive of our happiness. The punishment they receive is fully just

and fully embraced by Paolo and Francesca. He seems to be getting seriously off track in his course of studies!

124   Even though it hurts to remember, the lovers can't stop themselves from discussing the way it all happened.

127   As is the case with so many sins against purity, Paolo and Francesca's sin began almost innocently—a married woman and her handsome brother-in-law reading tales of courtly love alone together (well, that is perhaps not the most prudent way to spend a lonely, rainy afternoon with an attractive member of the opposite sex). Reading about Lancelot and Guinevere's affair, "We went pale, as we caught each other's glance." But, even then, there was the possibility of turning away. But on they read until they were imitating what they were reading. They spread their wings like the starlings in the wind. "That day we did not read another page." Need we say more?

> DEEP inside of our hearts, we know that we are supposed to act in accordance with principles. We know that we are not created to give in to every desire we experience. We recognize that caving in to our passions is a sign of weakness, and weakness is distinctly unattractive. To cover up this uncomfortable awareness, we try to place blame somewhere else, anywhere else. The devil made me do it! Anything to avoid the brutal honesty expressed so memorably by Oscar Wilde: "I can resist anything except temptation!"

137 They blame the book; they blame the author, accusing him of being a panderer or pimp—anything but taking responsibility for their own actions. They are victims to the end.

It is interesting that only Francesca speaks. This sort of victimhood would be far less appealing coming from a man. Paolo merely stands by silently as she makes excuse after excuse for their fall into lust.

140 Dante is so overwhelmed that he loses consciousness. So much for manly strength! Lust has the power to make him lose his senses. He has been defeated, even humiliated, by the power of the leopard.

CANTO 6

The Beastliness of Undirected Passion
Pitying What We Ourselves Have Experienced
The Holiness of Our Bodies

Passions are present in us for a reason. We have a desire for sex in order to assure the continuance of the human race. We desire food to help ensure proper nutrition for our bodies. These desires are natural and healthy in themselves, but they become destructive and dehumanizing when they no longer operate within their proper limits. Few sins display their beastliness for the entire world to see as vividly as gluttony. We might successfully hide our lustful affairs from sight, but the effects of overeating are harder to conceal. Perhaps they are also less likely to be glamorized.

1   Again, Dante is transported while unconscious. He doesn't get himself out of the circle of the lustful under his own power; he doesn't have the personal strength for that. He needs to be taken out of it—delivered—by

divine power. Like the lovers, he is passive. In our battle against powerful habits of sin, we are often so weakened that we need to be delivered by an external power, like the donkey that has collapsed under the burden he is carrying. We travel so far into the dark wood that we cannot get out of it on our own.

7   Here the mood is set by the continual rain. The rain is cold, mind-numbingly the same, and makes the ground stink. As a punishment for gluttony, however, the rain needs some explaining.

First, the rain itself. Rain is a necessity, a blessing from God, but once it is beyond the proper amount, it becomes a curse. In the same way, the gluttonous have taken food, a gift from God, something necessary for life, and abused it beyond any proper proportion. The image is of way too much of a good thing.

Second, the cold. Food is meant to nourish us, and metabolism warms the body. The comfortable warmth after a good meal is now something denied the gluttonous. Food wasn't used for its proper end, and here that end is never enjoyed.

Finally, the stink. Food, which is supposed to produce health, is far from healthy when taken in excess. A source of life becomes a source of corruption. Here the rain, rather than cleansing the ground, makes it fouler than it was before.

13 Cerberus, the three-headed dog, is a fitting beast to preside in the circle of the gluttonous. The mouths of the

gluttonous are always calling for more. He has three, which should make the truly gluttonous envious. He treats the souls punished here as food, "shred[ding] the souls to bits."

19 Again, we see the beastliness of sin. The souls howl like dogs in the rain, rolling on the ground, first on one side, then on the other, to protect themselves from the downpour. Gluttony is particularly beastly, without the glamorous and romantic overtones which so often let us gloss over the twistedness of lust. The continuous barking of Cerberus makes the souls punished there "wish that they could go deaf" (33). He is a constant, audible reminder of their abandonment of the paths of reason.

25 Virgil doesn't bother with commands by the authority of heaven or words of explanation to silence Cerberus, who doesn't seem to merit so much rational consideration. It is not necessary. Cerberus is easily manipulated. Virgil merely throws mud into his mouths. In his greed, the dog is entirely indiscriminate in his eating: "Yammering in an agony of greed . . ." This is junk food taken to the extreme. Notice that it is desire for the act of eating, rather than desire for nourishing food (which is perfectly natural), that is the driving force here. The passion for eating has made the gluttonous souls lose sight of the purpose of eating.

35 The gluttonous get the same sort of consideration as Cerberus did. Dante and Virgil actually walk on them:

they "fixed our soles upon what seemed their persons, but was emptiness." What is left of them is almost not identifiably human. They have consciously rejected their own dignity. Now they only seem to be animals rather than persons.

37   The prone position of the souls is an image of how low they have been brought down by their sin. They are in the mud face-first, like pigs wallowing in mire. The pig imagery will continue with the soul they address, Ciacco, whose very name means "hog."

40   Here again we see the desire that the damned souls have to be remembered, even in their horribly corrupted state: "Look at me well." In the emptiness of the gluttonous, their earthly fame is the most real thing about them, even if that memory is fundamentally negative. The desire to be remembered outweighs any sense of shame they might have at being associated with such a distasteful sin.

> PITY does not seem to be a very accurate emotion. We often bestow our pity upon very undeserving recipients. What moves us to a sympathetic reaction? Often, we identify personally with the sufferings we observe; they strike close to home. It is easier to put ourselves in someone else's shoes when we have experienced something similar in our own lives. After a battle with cancer, we work for the Cancer Society so that other people will not have to go through what we endured. What we find

> ourselves feeling pity for is often a manifestation of our own interior woundedness.

48   Dante certainly doesn't seem to experience pity here, does he? If it were merely the *suffering* of the souls of the lustful that moved him to pity and made him swoon at the end of the previous canto, you'd expect that same pity here even more because the suffering is greater. But that certainly isn't what we observe. Because Dante isn't personally involved in this particular sin, he can look upon it with full objectivity. What he sees is the deformity of the sin with none of its alluring disguises. With a conscience clear of the habit of gluttony, he sees it accurately, in all its unpleasantness.

49   Ciacco's first words are filled with images of the gluttony for which he suffers: "Your city, so stuffed full with envy that the sack's mouth spews it up . . ."

53   Ciacco presents his sin far more honestly than did Francesca in the previous circle. There seems less self-deception here. It is less possible to glamorize gluttony, even to ourselves, while lust so often disguises itself in the noble garb of love.

64   The souls in hell seem to have been given a special knowledge of the future. Often, they will prophesy to Dante about events in Florence. We'll see more about the strange knowledge these souls have, a knowledge that rather strangely does not include the present.

88   Ciacco wants to be remembered in the world. This desire lies at the root of the damned souls' desire to talk to Dante. He is going back to the world and can take word of these souls back. They want to be remembered: it is the only sort of positive immortality to which they can look forward.

94   Ciacco's only reason for speaking and acting was Dante's presence. Once Dante and Virgil have left, he'll be silent in the rain until the final judgment. The social aspects of food have entirely disappeared. Gluttony is a solitary action; it requires no words. The mouth is otherwise engaged.

> The Christian belief in the resurrection of the body ought to mean that we treat our bodies (and the bodies of others) with a special sort of respect. They are not disposable or exchangeable. They are somehow ours forever, an essential part of who we are. They are temples of the Holy Spirit. But this respect should manifest itself more immediately than the resurrection of the body. Already in this life, Christians pay attention to those sins called the "sins of the flesh." We do this not because we think that bodies are sinful. Christ's incarnation forces Christians away from a dualistic rejection of material bodies. We take these sins seriously because we consider our bodies something holy.

106   The resurrection of the body brings man to completion. He was created as a composite of body and soul.

His soul is intended to be in a body. Getting our bodies back at the general judgment makes us "more" of a being, more complete, which means more joy, but also more pain. Whatever state the soul "enjoyed" before the resurrection is now shared with the body. The souls in hell will be more "perfect" in their sufferings, just as the joy in heaven will be complete after the resurrection. Whatever sort of being the soul has, it will share with its body.

115   With Plutus, the god of wealth, we come across another demonic beast, showing what unbridled passion does to our humanity. He is our introduction to the next canto and circle of hell. Here we find the avaricious and the prodigal, those whose desire for or relation to money was disordered.

CANTO 7

Money, the Root of All Evils
The Spiritual Futility of Sin
Detachment, Not Deprivation
The Ferocious Grip of Anger

Catholic theologians always include lust and avarice in the list of sins that will be responsible for destroying the spiritual lives of the most souls. In one of his maxims, Saint Philip Neri taught, "Let the young man be on guard against the flesh and the old man against avarice, and we shall all be saints together" (3 November). Lust is the perversion of our most basic and powerful passion; it is easy to see how it captures so many souls. But avarice has its own appeal. Money gives us the means to indulge our passions; with it, we can buy what we desire. For this reason, Saint Paul writes, "For the love of money is the root of all evils" (1 Tm 6:10). Because of the power that money gives, the ungoverned desire for money can produce in us a vicious brutality, an "eat or be eaten" mentality. Families have fallen apart, friendships have been abandoned, legal contracts broken, and countries betrayed through the love of money. Avarice can bring out the beast in any of us.

1 *"Pape Satan, pape Satan aleppe!"* These are Plutus's words at Dante's entry to the fourth circle of hell. Much discussion has been given to whether they are meaningful or merely gibberish. Whatever the precise meaning (if any), the words seem to suggest that Plutus, the god of wealth (actually a demon), is giving some sort of tribute to Satan. Wealth so often is an instrument of evil—not evil in itself, but insofar as it makes evil, often great evil, possible. It is in this way, says St. Thomas, that money is the root of evil—because it provides the *means*.

Plutus might be a servant of Satan, giving honor to his master, but he is also a stupid servant, as his "clucking voice" suggests, preferring material goods to the truly human and lasting immaterial ones he was created for. He might be called a "god," but he is distinctly less than human. He deserves to speak gibberish.

3 Virgil, "aware of all," again recognizes the need to strengthen Dante's resolve. Even though our location hasn't been explained yet explicitly, we are entering the circle of the avaricious, avarice being a sin with which Dante struggled. The she-wolf, symbolizing avarice and greed, was the last of the three beasts that prevented Dante from climbing up the hill towards the light and out of the dark woods, the one who finally

made him give up his climb. Here in this circle, therefore, Dante will encounter another *bête noire*. His first encounter, in the circle of the lustful, was not particularly successful. Dante was so overcome with sympathy that he lost consciousness. Virgil is reminding Dante of the need for both courage and trust in his own particular spiritual battles.

8   Virgil handles Plutus rudely: "Shut up, you cursed wolf of Hell!" Wisdom has little respect for the unbridled desire for wealth. This is also a reminder of the natural supremacy reason has over the passions. This tone of voice is used consistently by Virgil when dealing with the beastly personifications of passion.

13 Notice that the beast, like the others, has no choice but to obey Virgil's voice, the voice of reason, the voice the passions were created to obey. Virgil announces God's will, and the demons of hell are immediately defeated; they fall silent at the command of reason. That is the very nature of passion—they are made for following the command of reason.

So often the wealthy are puffed up with pride, with a sense of their supposed importance and influence, like a sail filled with wind. How quickly that influence and importance can all disappear when the money goes. Dante, in exile and stripped of most of his possessions, knows that better than most. We shall observe this same image of being puffed up in the souls of both the avaricious and the squanderers.

CANTO 7

16   Notice that even before we officially know who is punished in this circle of hell, the imagery has already prepared us. First, Plutus, the god of wealth; now, the imagery of a purse that "bags all the evil of the universe." Dante allows his imagery to lead the way, to set the tone, before he actually explains with words. The imagery anticipates.

19   Dante's first reaction is one of surprise at the strangeness of the punishment here. Only God could have thought up such things. Unlike in the circle of the lustful, Dante, instead of being overwhelmed by pity, recognizes God's justice at work. Is that merely because he does not yet understand what sin is being punished here? Perhaps this sin of avarice, despite its attraction, is not so easy to glamorize as lust was.

> SIN is always a desire for a disordered good. This does not mean that the thing we desire is simply "against the rules." It is not something that will truly satisfy our desires. It might taste good, but it will not nourish us. Desiring these disordered objects is rather like accelerating down a dead-end street: it is both a dangerous thing to do and a futile one. Where does it get us? It is a great deal of work to achieve something that will not fulfill our desire. Sin is an exercise in spiritual futility. Avarice is a particularly exhausting sin that never allows a soul to rest.

23   The imagery is of collision—of the currents of the

ocean at the whirlpool of Charybdis in the straits of Messina, and later of the collisions of riders in jousting matches. There is a built-in conflict when people compete in an unrestricted manner for the finite material goods this world has to offer. There is only so much to go around. Trying to grab it for ourselves will always include running up against the desires, and perhaps the needs, of others. There is a sort of justice concerning these material goods our world has to offer, what the tradition calls "distributive justice." If we do not consider what money is really *for*, society will be condemned to a constant battle for wealth.

27. ". . . popping their chests to roll enormous weights." The men become beasts of burden, using their own chests, the very center of their bodies, to roll these stones. They throw their whole selves into their work. Where your heart is, there is also your treasure. In their earthly life, these men have spent themselves and their human dignity in the pursuit of material goods, and so here they are like cogs in a machine, making the wheels turn. The "popping their chests" makes them seem *proud*, proud of what is, ironically, a demeaning activity.

> A Christian is not necessarily called to a life of deprivation (thanks be to God!), but we are called to a state of detachment. We are to live in the world without becoming attached to it; we are to use the things of the world without clinging to them. We do not think that money

> is something evil; we need it to make life possible, we need it if we are to be generous with others. But money is merely a means to an end. We are to use it in such a way that we grow in charity and move closer to heaven.

30 Here, the sinners are participating in the punishment of one another. There are misers tormenting spendthrifts, and vice versa. Here, for the first time, we see two different extremes of the same desire. Often passions are indulged in only one direction—many people overeat, but, aside from the psychologically afflicted, the opposite extreme is very rare. But money has produced two very different camps of abusers: those who use it too much and those who hoard it and refuse to spend. Despite being opposites, both are materialists and both mistake the true meaning of material possessions. Virtue, as Aristotle tells us, is in the mean, in moderation. The imagery of Scylla and Charybdis is fitting here. The sailor must manage to steer his boat between the rocks and the whirlpool. Erring to either side would be his destruction.

The "dismal circle" reminds us of the drudgery in giving over one's life to the pursuit of money. This is the medieval version of the "rat race."

36 Here we get the first real indication of the personal toll this circle takes on Dante: "My heart was nearly pierced." He is a fellow sufferer, someone who is still attached to material things, especially those unjustly taken from him because of his exile.

39 The tonsured heads tell us that avarice is a problem for those who have come into positions of leadership in the Church. The Church needs money for its mission, but not merely in order to accumulate material goods and to enrich those who have been called to serve, not to be served. Vocations in the Church have been abused as *means* of ambition, both social ambition and financial ambition. For many, a vocation in the Church was a way, often the *only* way, to an education and a guaranteed income. This income grows as the person is promoted in the Church: thus financial ambition is the source of ecclesiastical ambition as well. See line 48: "Avarice browbeats, bullying to the top." It turns out that it has bullied them to the pit instead.

43 Both of these versions of materialists are portrayed as irrational—"their voices yap." They haven't ordered the lesser goods to the higher ones. They lack the true discernment that reason should bring.

52 The people here are faceless, their likeness dimmed "beyond recognition." Those who dedicate themselves to the pursuit of wealth, the "nothing-knowing life," especially *men*, often choose to identify themselves so much with their work that they have little personal identity left. They have chosen to subordinate their true personal dignity to their careers. Think of the men who, when asked "who are you?" will respond by telling you what they do. They've allowed themselves

CANTO 7

to become cogs in the machine, mere means of production (how Marxist!).

64 Money seems to be able to buy most things, but not what really matters. These souls would give all they had on earth for a moment's rest, a rest that will never come.

76 God's intention in granting material goods to creation is that they be available to all, "distributing the splendor equally"—what is called the "universal destination of goods." The ups and downs of fortune, Virgil explains, keep these goods from getting into one set of hands permanently. We are called to be stewards, not permanent owners; servants, not masters. Dante feels these cruel ups and downs particularly sharply—he's lost everything. Unfair though his fate may seem, it has forced him to work at being detached from material goods.

> ASIDE from lust, few passions can be so overwhelming as anger. It bursts through our defenses with almost volcanic force and blinds our reason. And its power is lingering, sometimes even growing with time. We store our anger away and nourish it by reviewing our grievances; each time we remember, we relive and rehearse the emotions, cultivating a grudge or long-standing bitterness. We human beings seem to have an enormous capacity for holding on to our anger. And nothing is more destructive of our own peace of mind. As Saint

> Philip told his followers, "He who continues in anger, strife, and a bitter spirit, has a taste of the air of hell" (6 September).

100 Next we are introduced to the second of the classical rivers of the underworld: Styx. It begins with a spring that "boiled and bubbled over," flowing with dark water, "purplish black." It is a river of boiling blood, a vivid image of the wrath or rage that we will discover is punished here. Again, we experience the image before we know what it signifies.

110 The boiling blood produces a muddy marsh into which these souls are immersed to varying degrees. Here we see anger beyond the control of reason—what we would call "blind rage." These souls use all they have, even their teeth, as weapons. Everything is used in the cause of their anger. This theme of sin as "obsession" is recurrent. These sinners set up their sin as the focus of their lives, whether that sin is lust, food, wealth, or anger. As the avaricious used their whole bodies to roll their weights around the dismal circle, the wrathful use their whole selves to vent their anger.

118 The bubbles in the marsh tell us that some souls, souls whose rage was even greater than that of the others, are entirely submerged in the mud. What we see of wrath is often the lesser part. Much of it happens "beneath the surface," attacking in secret. Much of the nastiness we experience in the world is under cover.

121 These souls are "stuck in the mire," a nice image of the way anger takes hold of us and won't let go, like a foot caught in mud or even quicksand. Their hearts smolder, "bearing a sluggish smoke within our hearts." Anyone who has experienced resentment will recognize the aptness of the description.

129 It seems as though the wrathful souls are trying to nourish themselves with their anger. They treat the wrongs done to them as treasures to be guarded and protected, as a delicacy to be enjoyed. It reminds us of the old saying that vengeance is a dish that is best served cold, or, perhaps more aptly, that resentment is like drinking poison and waiting for the other person to die.

CANTO 8

Anger, the Door to Unexpected Sins
Battle Against Our Most Besetting Sins
Hell as a Prison
Breaking Through Hardness of Heart

Our anger, especially if we allow it to ferment and fester, transports us to other sins. It signals us to contemplate revenge, calling either violence or deceit into service to attain its goal. Our anger opens the doors to actions we would never otherwise even consider. Is there anything we would not do when we are beside ourselves with rage? "The anger of man does not work the righteousness of God" (Jas 1:20). It serves a very different master.

5   Dante and Virgil observe a signal tower that is transmitting, but what signal is it sending, and to where, to whom? As soon as they see signaling, they immediately arrive at some rather unpleasant conclusions.

         The most obvious conclusion, at least from the

comfort of our reading chair, and especially if we scan ahead a few lines, is that the lights signal that there is a passenger ready to cross the river they are approaching, the river Styx. It is merely a signal for the ferry to carry Virgil and Dante across to the other side. But there might be a more sinister meaning of the signal, and since this is hell, more sinister interpretations seem quite fitting. The hellish hosts are preparing themselves, marshalling their forces to defend their city against these unidentified intruders. As it turns out, both conclusions turn out to be valid.

19   Phlegyas is yet another of the keepers of hell who are silenced at Virgil's command. Virgil's words are rather hard to interpret at first: "You'll have us only while we cross the slough." Phlegyas had thought he recognized in Dante a soul that belonged in his river. With his spiritual sight, he reads Dante's soul: "Traitor! I've got you now, you wicked soul!" He does not ask what they are doing there. Virgil tells him, however, that he will not have Dante permanently, but only for as long as it takes to cross the river. As we shall see, Filippo Argenti saw the same spiritual reality in Dante.

27   Dante weighs down the boat; Virgil doesn't. Dante's bodiliness stands out.

33   "... who come before your hour." We've seen already that Dante's reactions to various areas of hell tell us something about the state of his soul. Dante swoons with the lustful because he fights against the same

temptation; he is a "fellow sufferer." Here we are given another clue to Dante's spiritual state, one that will continue to be used throughout the *Purgatorio* as well: the souls recognize him as belonging with them, being one of them. The souls seem to have a spiritual power of discernment, and one of them discerns that Dante belongs here in the circle of the wrathful.

35 The exchange between Dante and the soul in the river, Filippo Argenti, is as ill-tempered as you would expect in the circle of the wrathful. Dante displays no real sympathy, but recognizes the basic ugliness of the sin: "But who are you, made ugly by such filth?" Dante is not deceived here. He sees the sin for what it truly is: deformed and ugly. This is very different from his reaction to the souls of the lustful, whom Dante mistakenly thinks suffer because of "love." He gets caught up with the romantic disguise and misses the deformity underneath.

> IN the spiritual life, there are so very many battles that need to be fought, sooner or later. But we need to direct our energies where they are needed most urgently, without being distracted by the less insistent issues. We need to work like a triage nurse in an emergency room, looking through all the symptoms that the patient presents for the conditions that are currently most threatening. Where we discern a strong attachment to sin, there serious work needs to be done right away. Aside from the rather obvious tactic of avoiding the occasions of sin,

> fostering a vivid hatred for the sin is one of our most powerful spiritual weapons. We need to build up in ourselves the drive to fight the good fight against our besetting sins, because it will be a fight.

44   "Indignant soul!" Virgil throws his arms around Dante, kisses him, and praises him for his harsh treatment of this soul that rises from the Styx to confront him. Why such an enthusiastic reaction? Something important for Dante's journey must be happening here.

      Dante previously has been corrected for pitying too much the state of the damned (especially the lustful)—the one exception is for the souls in Limbo, and Virgil has a personal (not entirely objective) reason for encouraging Dante's pity there. Here Virgil rewards Dante's lack of pity. If Dante *is* one of them, someone filled with anger (remember the lion, with its pride and wrath), then an important and much neglected step in his spiritual conversion is the development of a true *hatred of the sin*, a recognition of the damage the sin causes. Dante needs to begin to see sin as it really is rather than being fooled by the many pleasant disguises it wears. He needs to view it as something to be fought at all costs.

52   Dante recognizes the soul himself and the justice of the soul's being submerged in the filthy waters of Styx. Here what might seem like anger is not a sin, but righteous indignation, like Christ in the temple. We have to be ready to enter into the spiritual combat, and that

requires both the spiritual discernment to see sin as it is and also the courage to fight against it. In both of these ways Dante has so often been lacking. Here he shows real spiritual progress, and Virgil is quick to affirm him in his righteous desire. "Such a desire is good to satisfy."

> The perfect happiness of the City of God is mirrored in a horrible way by the dystopia that is hell. Heaven is made blessed by the vision of God and our perfect union with him. Hell is defined by his permanent absence. Despite the alluring disguise of sin, there is nothing splendid or free or glorious about Satan's kingdom. It is a prison on lockdown.

68 ". . . the city they call Dis." We've traveled from the outer walls of the city (the anti-Jerusalem, the mirror-image of the City of God) to the inner walls, the citadel, with guarded gates and watchtowers. The towers are like the minarets of mosques: the culture wars certainly aren't anything new.

74 The heavenly Jerusalem glows with the gold and jewels of which it is constructed. There the glory fills the streets, but here the glow comes from fire, like the glowing furnaces of a forge. The heavenly Jerusalem has seven gates and all who truly desire it might enter. The kingdom of sin is much more "closed off," with iron walls and moats protecting it from intrusion— but by whom? The iron walls make the city seem

almost impossible to penetrate. Natural powers are at a loss here; there appears to be no way in.

82 The walls are "manned" by fallen angels. As angels stand in the presence of God in heaven, here they perform a similar function for Satan.

> OUR reasoning and our entreaties can sometimes move the hearts of those who are disastrously attached to sin, especially if we have a profound connection with them. They are conflicted people; part of them still recognizes and responds to the truth we are presenting and the connection we are offering. But the embittered, hardened person is often unmoved by our words, even scornful of them. Their hearts have become hearts of stone, and only God can transform them into hearts of flesh again. For some reason, some very sad reason, they have become fortified against the world and their neighbors.

89 The fallen angels don't respond immediately to Virgil's requests. They command *him*. He seems to recognize that he is in over his head. He asks to speak with them over to the side, alone. They respond with threats that Virgil will be held there and Dante will have to find his way back by himself. Why don't they obey Virgil like the beasts and demons who were in the circles punishing sins of passion? The hardness of heart that comes with malice is the root of the explanation, as will become clearer in the next canto. These demons are no longer open to the appeals of reason.

94 They seem intent upon inspiring despair in Dante's heart, and do quite a good job of it. Virgil tries to reassure him but can only say that he won't leave Dante alone. He doesn't explain a plan; he doesn't seem to have one.

115 Virgil's attempt to talk his way into Dis fails miserably. The gates of the city are slammed in his face. He is obviously bewildered himself. We are accustomed to Virgil having all the answers, solving all the problems, but here "his eyes were bowed to earth, his brow was shorn of all his boldness as he sighed and said, 'Who are these here to block my going down?'" His powers seem to be useless here. What can he do?

125 Virgil places his hope, not in his own powers, but in his *experience* of previous victory over the forces of evil—the harrowing of hell, when Christ broke open the gates of hell itself. We've already seen some of the effects of divine power in hell. The gates are off their hinges, landslides disfigure the landscape.

Note that hope comes from experience; otherwise, it is empty wishful thinking. Hope needs to have a foundation, and that foundation is an awareness of how things have worked in the past. This is why it is easier for the young to experience despair; they haven't lived enough, and seen enough, to have a solid foundation for hope. When hope falters, we need to draw our minds back to those previous victories and consolations that we have experienced. Hope is fostered by reflection and thanksgiving. As we'll see, Virgil's hope is not in vain.

CANTO 9

Trust in God as a Last Resort
Our Need for Support in the Spiritual Life
Our Frustrating Lack of Progress
A Humble Heart and a Believing Intellect

Exercising and developing the virtue of trust is almost always an unpleasant experience. When we feel confident that everything will work out as we hope, when we can see how it will happen, when we think we can count on our own strength, there is really no need for trust at all; we are merely being self-reliant, not reliant on God. Trusting in God is very often a last resort for us, something to which we turn when we have already tried and exhausted every other option. Perhaps this helps explain why God allows us these moments of intense vulnerability and panic in our lives; it is only in them and through them that we can grow in trust.

1   Dante is afraid, but he isn't alone in his fear. Virgil has gone pale as well, which does nothing to encourage

Dante. Virgil catches himself when he realizes the effect his own worry is having on Dante.

7   We can hear the uncertainty in Virgil's voice. He stammers, unable to complete his thought. He tries to reassure himself—we see him struggling to trust. We *must* win, but what if not? We have such great help on our side, but why is the help so long in coming? Hope is always for something we don't yet have; it is never easy and comfortable. Much of this canto focuses on the need for trust—not just for a journey through hell, but on the spiritual journey that every human being must make. Holding on to hope is the battle. After all, "abandon hope" is inscribed above the gates of hell for a reason. We must hold on to hope if we want to stay out of hell.

16   Dante seems to be changing the subject, finding something to talk about to cover up their mutual fears, but that is only an appearance. He is really trying to ask Virgil in a roundabout way whether he knows what he is doing.

    His words only focus more sharply on hope. Has anyone ever done this before? Is it really possible? This is why people who suffer want to hear from others who have gone through similar trials and so form "support groups." They want to know that victory is *possible*, that they aren't alone on this path. That is why people experience such relief reading spiritual books that accurately describe their own struggles and inner battles. They aren't so strange; they aren't alone.

> HUMAN beings are social by nature. We need community. And this need for support and guidance is felt most keenly when we are struggling. When we realize that we have lost our way and are beginning to panic interiorly, the calm voice of someone we trust is like salve on a painful wound. The painful experience of learning that we cannot trust ourselves pushes us towards trusting in God. Distrust of self and trusting in God grow along side of one another. Only someone who knows the pain of feeling lost, of distrusting his own sense of direction, is truly ready to ask to be shown the way.

30 "I know the journey well." Virgil has made this trip before, shortly after his death. He was summoned to retrieve a soul from the pit of hell. He has been there and back again.

On a difficult journey, we want an experienced guide, not a theory, and that is precisely how Virgil presents himself to Dante. From sitting at the feet of philosophers or spiritual gurus, to obeying personal trainers or athletic coaches, human beings want *someone* wise whom they can trust, someone who can show them the way. We want a *person* to follow. Remember canto 1, 136: "He set on, and I held my pace behind," or canto 2, 139: "Go, for we two now share one will alone: you are my guide, my teacher, and my lord."

Our Lord himself knows our human need: he didn't just teach a theory—he said, "Follow me."

37   Here we are presented with the three Furies from Greek tragedy. They are horrible instruments of justice, pursuing those who have sinned grievously and driving them to either repentance or madness. They are a force of nature, unrelenting, not someone with whom you argue or negotiate in a calm and rational manner. Their presence announces the seriousness of the sins punished within Dis and are another example of Dante's blending mythology and Christian teaching.

52   "Medusa, come!" The Gorgon (Medusa) can turn anyone who looks at her to stone. The journey would be over; life would be over; there would be no chance for Dante to get things right.

The spiritual significance might be that we all have the potential, especially when dealing with certain sorts of sins, to get hardened into place, leaving no room for change or conversion. "If today you here his voice, harden not your hearts." "For should you see the Gorgon if she shows, there would be no returning above!" When fighting against sins of passion, there is still a part of us, our reason, with which we can do battle. Reason works at commanding the passions (as Virgil has commanded the beasts of hell), gradually habituating them to obey. So long as reason is operational, the possibility of subduing the passions remains.

But what happens when reason itself becomes infected? What weapons are available for battle then? Sins that involve reason are the hardest to cure. Since reason is part of the problem, because it is already contaminated by sin, it cannot be helpful in the cure. Something from the outside seems to be necessary, something supernatural.

This explains why Virgil, as the voice of reason, has no power to command here in the realm where reason itself has been eternally corrupted.

58   "Since he did not trust my own . . ." When fighting against temptations, very often we fail because we trust our own power, our own ability to turn away, to say no at the last minute. We walk up to the very edge of the cliff, saying that we will not fall. We enjoy the experience of being tempted, and we think we are strong enough to back away from the pull of the temptation at the final moment. But experience teaches us a very different lesson, and so does Dante's meeting with the Gorgon. Virgil doesn't trust Dante, even with his eyes closed, even with his hands over his eyes. Virgil covers Dante's hands with his own. Remember St. Philip's maxim: "I trust in Thee, but not in me." Is that the lesson that the clear intellects Virgil speaks about are supposed to take? When reason is part of the problem, we must be very aware of our ability to deceive ourselves, to rationalize. Covering the eyes is a sign of the untrustworthiness of our knowing power with this sort of sin.

> PROGRESS in the spiritual life often does not happen at the pace we would like. We want results, measurable results, something to show for our efforts. The harder we work, the greater the result; that seems only reasonable. But often our efforts seem to produce nothing of value. We seem as impatient as ever; sometimes it seems as if we are growing worse instead of improving! This apparent powerlessness to fight effectively against sin results in frustration and even despair. But the power of God can achieve in a moment what we have been working toward for years. Our efforts are not useless. They are essential, but they are not enough on their own. God wants us to be very clear about that. No one hikes his way into heaven by his own strength.

79 See how the powers of hell scatter at the presence of a heavenly power. The wrathful souls in the river submerge like frightened frogs, and the fallen angels simply disappear. The angel walks on the water of the river, wiping away the grimy fog from in front of his face. This image is taken over by C. S. Lewis in his *Great Divorce*. There the bus driver taking the souls from the grey town to heaven does the same thing. In the angel's manner, there is almost a scorn for the messiness of sin.

89 At the mere wave of his wand, the angel ends the rebellion. There is no dramatic battle, no heroic conflict: he waves his "little wand" and "there was nothing to resist." Dante carefully diminishes the true power of

hell; their power is only an illusion, at least for those who remain in God's grace. The littleness of the wand shows how insignificant this particular battle is for the host of heaven. The angel makes the futility of their struggle explicit: "Why do you kick your heels against the will of Him whose ends can never be cut short?" He heads off almost bored—with "other business on his mind." So much for dualism: good and evil are obviously not equals in the battle.

112 The tombs here are pushed this way and that—almost haphazard, as in places very near the water. The sense is of the tombs being treated with a sort of lack of respect. This sense of abandonment and disregard is heightened by the flames present in each tomb, heating them red-hot, like forges. Whatever these tombs are, they aren't resting places.

> OUR faith arises not from an intellectual grasp of the truths of faith but from our own personal experience of the love of God. Because of that experience, we trust him and all that he tells us. If this is why we begin to believe, then why do some people stop? Why do they get off track about the faith? The explanation is not mainly intellectual; it happens because of a break in our trusting relationship with God. These failures of faith become heretical movements in the Church when we become obstinate in our erroneous opinions, when we gather into party factions for support in our views, when we pit one side against another. Underneath heresy is not a confused intellect but a rebellious heart.

127 Christians become followers of Christ by baptism. By being united with him in his death and burial, we come to share also in his resurrection. Heretics set themselves up as "other Christs," and their followers have gone after them rather than Christ. These followers, some of

whom we will meet in the next canto, are buried with their leaders, but there will be no rising to new life. They have sided with them rather than with Christ and his Church. But Christ alone has given us victory over the grave—"I will call you from your tombs." The heretics have merely given their followers tombs. Each tomb contains a different heresy, a sort of parody of the communion of the saints, crammed together in their punishment.

CANTO 10

True Belief as the Guide to Good Action
Our Spiritual Selves
The Stubborn Unwillingness to Admit We Are Wrong
Living in the Present Moment

Modern Christians, in order to foster some semblance of unity, often seem to promote the notion that what we believe does not really matter, so long as we try to be good to one another. But true belief does matter. As human beings, our actions are supposed to be governed by our reason. If we do not know the truth, our actions will be misguided, which is very sad. But if we were willingly to reject the truth, we would be abandoning any chance of fulfilling our human responsibility. We cannot expect people to act well when they are convinced of wrongful beliefs. Our modern world gives us a horrible selection of examples from which we can illustrate this truth.

1   In keeping with the idea that hell is a sort of upside-down

city of heaven, notice that here the tombs are just *inside* the city walls. In most cities, tombs would be outside, considered something unclean. Here the entrance to the city is in fact the cemetery. This is yet another reminder that hell is absence of hope, a place where our hope dies.

10   At the time of the resurrection of the body, Christ promises us that he will raise us from our tombs. His being raised from the tomb is the ultimate guarantee that Our Lord is precisely who he claims to be: God, the source of all life. This victory over the grave, won for us by Christ, has been rejected by heretics, who have obstinately refused to submit themselves to his rule. As a sign of this rejection, their "victory" over the grave will be short-lived. When our bodies are liberated from the tomb at the time of the final judgment, the souls of the heretics will receive their bodies only to lead them back to the tomb and have their tombs sealed—permanently. They have rejected victory over the grave.

MATERIALISTS hold that material reality is the only reality. There is no spiritual soul; there is no life after death. This world is all that we have, and so we might as well enjoy it as much as we can. Materialism was a popular philosophy in the ancient world, but it has achieved even greater influence in our own day. Even those who identify themselves as Christians rarely seem to think about heaven. Heaven is more often than not merely a sort of insurance policy against death: if I have to die

> (and I'd rather not), then I hope there is a good place for me to go. How many people live with any awareness of the reality of their spirit and the eternal destiny to which they are called?

14   Epicurus is a Greek philosopher now associated primarily with a sort of hedonism. That is certainly inaccurate. He was a materialist, dedicated to the enjoyment of simple pleasures, but always in proper moderation. In more modern terms, the Epicureans could be seen as materialists, or secularists. There are no spiritual realities, no immortal soul. This world, the material world, is all that matters, all that is real. But regardless of his position, he is a *philosopher*. You'd expect him to be with the other Greek philosophers in limbo. Why is he here as our first personal example of heresy?

One can make an argument for Epicurus's being a heretic in two ways.

First, we are responsible for the foreseeable consequences of our actions. His philosophy has led others, Christians, into heresy, and he is responsible for that effect. Perhaps Dante focuses upon him because his philosophy had become popular among Dante's political foes, the Ghibellines. Farinata, whom we will meet soon, is a Ghibelline from Florence, but also an Epicurean.

There is a second way by which we can argue more directly that Epicurus himself is guilty of heresy; he somehow sins against the deposit of the faith, even though he isn't a believer. This is possible because the deposit of faith is composed not only of the mysteries of the faith but also of those truths we call preambles, truths necessary for our salvation but knowable by reason alone. The existence of some reality beyond the physical is a truth which reason should be able to establish but is also part of the deposit of the faith: it is a preamble. Epicurus, by being a bad philosopher, also manages to be a heretic. Epicurus's heresy must be more than merely making a *mistake* about a philosophical truth that is technically knowable by reason alone. Epicurus's being a heretic would require him to *know* the truth and to reject it with full awareness of what he was doing. Heresy requires full knowledge and full consent; it cannot be a matter of simple ignorance, unless that ignorance is itself culpable.

This inclusion of Epicurus here also gives special dramatic emphasis to Dante's discussion of the resurrection of the body. They are discussing the resurrection over the tomb of someone who denied the possibility of life after death.

28 Dante hears the voice addressing him but sees no one. That is the reason for his fear. Virgil is quick to correct Dante's fearfulness: "What are you doing? Turn around!" Later he will push Dante towards Farinata: "And with his prompt and spirited hand my guide / pushed me toward him among the sepulchers" (37–38). Dante's fear is constantly being challenged by

Virgil. He is pushed into the exercise of the virtue of courage.

> How stubborn we can be in holding to our opinions! We get defensive when contradicted by others and take a fighting posture. Even when we are faced with incontrovertible facts, we make excuses and arguments that no one can take seriously. So why do we fight for a position we must interiorly know to be wrong? Because it is ours. We are defending our own territory intellectually, no matter how foolish it makes us appear.

36 "... as if he held all Hell in scorn." This is an Epicurean speaking, someone who denies the reality of the afterlife. How *should* he react to hell he sees right there before his eyes? He intellectually rejects its existence but finds himself in the midst of it. He acknowledges Dante, a living being, but avoids any mention of the fact that his position has been proven wrong in the most obvious and dramatic way. He is *in* hell but denies the *existence* of the afterlife. Perhaps Dante intends this as a display of the obstinacy of heretics, stubbornly holding on to their position in contradiction to the obvious facts.

42 Farinata first asks Dante, with disdain, about Dante's family. Notice the focus on this world. Someone who believes that this life is all that there is sees our families as the only real source of immortality. The disdain Farinata shows Dante is probably on *political* grounds;

family associations and political associations are intimately wound up together. Remember, Farinata is both an Epicurean and a Ghibelline. No wonder he looks down on Dante.

43 Dante is *bold* here. There is vigor in his response. He does seem to be learning his lessons. He gives as good as he gets.

60 Perhaps the soul rising up to his chin, Cavalcante, recognizes Dante's living voice as the voice of the friend of his son, Guido the poet, and hopes that his son accompanies him on this journey through hell. If so, if Cavalcante is looking for his son to join him in this circle of hell, it would be ironic that an Epicurean should be hoping to see his son again after death—so much for not believing in the afterlife. Note also how both here and with Farinata, Dante emphasizes the hypocrisy of the Epicureans—their actions and the supposed denial of anything spiritual don't really fit together. It's hard to be a truly consistent materialist, especially as a spiritual soul living in hell. Their very existence is an overwhelming argument against their heresy.

77 The earthly fate of his family matters more to Farinata than his own eternal destiny. We see his heresy summed up in this one comment: his family's earthly suffering "wrings / more pain from me than does this bed of fire." There is no doubt that he still holds his materialist heresy.

82   "... to the sweet world." Again, Farinata's focus is on the earthly. But how common is this position of attachment to the material world even among those who call themselves believers. Think of the number of people who would do almost anything to stay alive, even if they had certainty about going to heaven. It's almost as though this world is the best thing: if you *have* to die, then heaven is to be preferred to hell—the lesser of two evils! Heaven rarely seems to be truly desired by those who call themselves believers.

> KEEPING our minds focused upon the present, upon what we need to do in this very moment, is a repeated maxim of the saints. Focusing upon the past only leads us to despair over what we cannot change. Setting our sights upon the future fills us with anxiety, since we have no control over it. The present is the only part of time that truly exists. It is all that we really have. God's eternity is described as an eternal present. The spiritual life demands that we train ourselves to live fully in the present moment.

97   Dante has seen the power of the damned souls to see the future. He assumes that their knowledge covers everything. But Farinata's question, and Cavalcante's before it, makes Dante realize that they cannot, however, know the present. The blessed in heaven see all things by seeing them in God, the eternal present; this "present" is all they need to know, for in knowing him,

they know everything. But the present is the one thing the damned cannot see. Because of this, Dante has something that souls in hell want: knowledge of the present. He will use this commodity to his advantage, doling out information when he needs something from the souls.

The strange knowledge of the damned is more than just a clever inversion of the beatific vision of the blessed in heaven who see all things in the all-present God; it is part of the punishment in hell. As time comes to an end, there is no more future, only the past and present. Those in hell are trapped entirely in the past, looking back at a life they can no longer enjoy. They are "petrified" in the past, while the blessed see all of time in God's *totum simul* existence. The life of the damned is narrowing, like the closing of the lid of the tombs of the heretics, while that of the blessed is opening out. "Evermore dead will be all our knowledge from the time the future ends, and Judgment shuts the door."

109 Dante's awareness of the state of knowledge of the damned moves him to compassion for Cavalcante; he is, after all, his friend's father. Dante wants him to know that his son Guido is still alive. Justice is making him suffer enough. Falsehood and deceit, even if unintended, should not be added to his burden. The punishments of hell are an action of justice, not cruelty.

118 Dante emphasizes the vast number of those who have

followed this materialist heresy. Here, at the beginning of the Renaissance, he already sees in his contemporary society the danger of focusing one's full attention on purely natural goods. In these thoughts and social criticisms, Dante seems more Medieval than Renaissance. But the life he has been living up until his journey to hell is definitely the life of a Renaissance poet. He seems to be calling into question this overarching focus on the human, the rational, and the worldly. And he does this by the simple literary device of giving his exclusive attention in this circle of the heretics to one heresy—that of the Epicureans.

CANTO 11

God's Providence at Every Moment
Every Sin's Victim
Truth as a Building Block of Society

God makes use of all things. Everything, even what we consider despicable and evil, becomes an element in his providential plan. God transforms Judas's betrayal, the plotting of the scribes and Pharisees, and Pontius Pilate's washing his hands of responsibility and remolds them into the means of our salvation. And every moment of time is useful as well. God has some function for our delays, our unexpectedly being stuck in traffic. He knows it is happening, and he has included it in his plan for us from all eternity. What spiritual use can we make of this moment?

1   These broken stones are yet another instance of the damage done in hell during Our Lord's descent. Hell is filled with visible reminders of the Saving Death of Christ and his power over death. The damage he left

behind in hell becomes a stepping stone for Dante on his journey.

2. We are told something important about the sins punished in the next areas of hell by the imagery. First, unlike the terraces that distinguish the different sins of the passions, here the next circle of hell is at the bottom of a "steep pit." Whatever sins are yet to come are

significantly different from what has come before, as symbolized by the physical distance we must travel to arrive at the circle. Second, the sins are characterized by an "overwhelming stink" which is so strong that it makes our travelers step back and wait until their sense of smell grows accustomed to it. Clearly, the sins punished here are particularly foul; they carry with them some sort of decay, something rotten to the core.

10   Even good people like Dante and Virgil grow accustomed to the odor of sin when given the opportunity. It offends at the beginning, it can even be overwhelmingly repulsive, but we grow used to it with time. This provides us with compelling reason to avoid the occasions of sin. We do not want to allow ourselves to become calloused to the evil our consciences perceive. The longer we stay around the sin, the greater the chance that we stop noticing the smell of decay.

13   It is good to see Dante taking the initiative. He is beginning to recognize that there is an urgency in his life; time is valuable. He needs to derive spiritual benefit from it.

> MODERN society has moved away from the criminalization of what many would call "victimless crimes." These crimes might involve consensual sex or drug use or any number of other hidden activities. But the argument is basically the same: it is not hurting anyone. But is that true? The Christian tradition would say no. There

> are no victimless crimes. Every sin damages the sinner, even if we gleefully pursue it. As God's creature, when we damage what he has made and loves, we offend him. The more profound the damage, the greater the offense. Whether or not these sins should be against the law is debatable, but we as Christians cannot lose sight of the fact that they are wrong and destructive. They are no less harmful or sad just because the harm is so often self-inflicted.

16   Virgil uses this time of acclimatizing to the smell to give Dante a sort of hellish geography lesson, describing in a systematic way the lay of the land of the remaining parts of hell. There is a logical ordering to hell based upon the destructive power of sin, destructive not only to those against whom we sin but primarily to ourselves. Sin destroys, or rots, the sinner. The greater and more incurable the damage to the sinner, the greater the sin. This intrinsic damage to the sinner's humanity is the underlying criterion for the organization of hell.

22   Virgil begins with the genus of all the remaining sins to be encountered in hell: malice, a type of sin that has injustice as its goal. All that follows is a subdivision of this. The genus of malice is divided into two species according to the instrument or means by which the malice is done: by force (or violence) or by fraud.

25   Dante considers fraud to be worse than violence. This position is perhaps a shock to modern sensibilities.

But the reason Virgil offers in explanation might be as perplexing as the statement itself: "since fraud's a sin peculiar to mankind." As we'll continue to see, Dante, in a way very unfamiliar to modern ears, judges the severity of a sin not so much by the damage it does to others, and certainly not by the damage it does to God (how can we hurt God?), but by the damage it does to our humanity. In this way of thinking, every sin has a victim; every sin harms someone: the sinners. Where is this spiritual rot? Is it relatively superficial, as in the case of the sins of the passions? The reason and will still remain whole and still have the opportunity to direct the passions. At the core of the person, there is still a force for good. This is why these sins are punished higher in hell; that is, less severely.

However, what about a sin that strikes more at the heart of what it means to be human? The sins that do are more serious. Malicious sins are a defect of the will itself, the will that is supposed to be the power that has command over the passions. How can things go right when the commanding power itself is corrupt? Fraud, even though it might seem to cause less damage to the outside world, is more destructive to the sinner himself. In fraud, reason itself is the instrument of sin, destroying the trust that is necessary for human society. Man, a social being, cannot exist without this network of connections.

35   Notice that violence against a person and violence against his property are punished together. This is a

very Christian and particularly medieval idea. The very foundation for the right of personal property is that having some basic amount of material goods is necessary to preserve both life and the freedom to decide how our lives are lived. If someone else owns what we need, we'll never be free. This is the justification of the Church's rejection of Communism. The dignity of the individual requires individual possession of property. To take someone's possessions, therefore, is to take something necessary for life. We can also see how our property is part of ourselves when we think about the change that happens in our lives when we have been the victims of robbery. Even if there was no violence against our person, we feel violated, our security shattered, our privacy stripped away.

40 Those who are violent against themselves are worse than those who are violent against others. Again, this is not a very modern view, as we increasingly move towards the sanctioning of a "right to die," a right to decide for ourselves when and how our life ends. The assumption is that our life belongs to us, and so we should be free in how we treat it and when we reject it. Taking someone else's life, however, is a violation of their freedom.

The key to understanding Dante's view is that it is far more basic to our humanity to respect our own life than to respect the life of others. If we don't value the life we have, a life of which we have firsthand experience, we'll never value the life of our neighbor. Suicide strikes closer to the core than homicide does; we have a natural desire for self-preservation.

Again, the same association of sins against a person and against his property holds true. Suicides and spendthrifts (who spend money in an extravagant, wasteful, or irresponsible way) are punished together; both have rejected the gift of life that was entrusted to them by God.

46   Violence against God is obviously not violence against God himself (because that is impossible), but against his creation and his will. We can sin by violence against God by acting against nature itself, or against nature's goods, or directly against God as he reveals himself. The "poster child" for sins against nature is sodomy in all its forms, turning what is supposed to be a life-giving action into something sterile. The usurer sins against nature's good by taking something that is supposed to be sterile (money) and trying to make it fertile. And blasphemers rage against God and his will directly. This ring, with its three subsets, would be almost entirely overlooked by the modern world with its existentialist rejection of any idea of a fixed human nature or of natures in general. If sins against nature are in fact sins of violence against God, then, as we see these sins against nature proliferate and even be accepted as normal by large segments of society, perhaps we should not be surprised to see a rise in anger against God and his religion and a corresponding rise in the persecution that results from that anger.

> LYING has become a standard practice in business and politics. Many people explore the boundaries of lying every time they fill out tax forms! Telling the truth seems like giving the competition an unfair advantage or giving the government more than it deserves. And so twisting the truth is something most everyone does. But what happens as a result of this general acceptance of lying? The bonds of trust are gradually weakened, and our relationships become increasingly adversarial. We become competitors rather than cooperators.

52   "Now fraud—which bites at every conscience . . ." This phrase seems open to several interpretations. First, it is something that everyone does. As a result, fraud is something by which every conscience ought to be bothered. Second, perhaps fraud gnaws at conscience in such a way that the fraudulent can't help but notice. We are using our reason to sin. How can we not notice? Or, finally, perhaps fraud "eats away" at conscience, gradually separating us from that sense of connectedness that helps to keep us on the right track? At the beginning, fraud is certainly something of which the sinner must be aware, but as time goes on, he seems to notice less and less. Recall Dante and Virgil gradually becoming accustomed to the stench at the edge of the pit of hell.

53   Fraud can either abuse the general trust that one human being should be able to have for another or it can abuse or violate a special bond of trust; for

example, that between friends or family members. The first is called simple fraud, and the latter, because it breaks a twofold bond, complex fraud. Fraud seems to be worse, according to Dante, than violence because it is more destructive of what it means to be human. When we take part in fraud in a consistent and habitual way, something inside of us dies. Our connection with our fellow man is broken. Violence might be able to be justified in other ways, but fraud is rotten to the core.

61   The more fundamental the bonds we betray, the worse is the fraud. There are bonds we have with any human being, precisely because we are sharers in human nature. But there are bonds which are more profound that give us a special connection to people, like family, friends, or guests. Betraying these bonds is a special act of treachery.

83   Incontinence, or sins of the passions, offend God to a lesser degree because they don't reach so deeply in man's nature. In these sins, the passions overwhelm reason. With sins of malice, the reason itself is the problem.

94   When Dante was writing, however, the understanding of money was developing rapidly. We are so accustomed to think of money as an asset like any other, something we can invest wisely ("make your money work as hard as you do," says one bank advertisement). Dante, as we'll see more of later, is noticeably more

old-fashioned than St. Thomas, for example, in this regard. For Dante, possessions come from "human industry," what we add to the value of things. Work is part of what we were called to do in the Garden of Eden. The Fall isn't the reason we have to work; it is merely the reason that work is considered burdensome.

CANTO 12

The Angry Roots of Violence
The Dehumanizing Power of Intimidation

The lines between anger and violence are often difficult to draw clearly. Anger is clearly a passion, but there seems to be something more than passion at work in an act of violence. Perhaps some violent acts are the result of overwhelming bursts of anger. But in most cases of violence, there is a point at which some sort of choice is made. The boiling blood of anger might incite the violence, but there is something more calculating and rational about it, something disturbingly human. Perhaps anger is the slippery slope down which many slide into violent behavior.

7   Notice that here the landscape has been markedly altered by the earthquake at the Crucifixion and the harrowing of hell.
    First, think about where we see these effects; where is the destruction most noteworthy? There seems to

be a correlation between the extent of the destruction and the relation that particular sins had to Our Lord's death. Violence was certainly a contributing factor. Pay attention to where the damage seems the worst, and see whether there is a pattern that develops.

Second, note that the landslide provides the passageway for Dante and Virgil to continue their journey. Our Lord's death provides the "way" for us to make progress on the journey towards salvation in the same way that it gave Dante and Virgil a way of climbing down to the next circle of hell. "Such was the way to go down this gorge here" (10).

12 The circles of sins of passion, through which we have already passed, were dominated by beastly imagery. There were beasts guarding the circles (like Cerberus), and the sinners themselves were often described in beastly terms, especially the gluttonous, who wallowed like pigs.

This circle, the circle of the violent, is dominated by the half-beastly figures of the minotaur and centaurs. These half-men half-beasts remind us that when we give ourselves over to violence, we are choosing, as rational beings, to act like beasts. Our reason and our anger work together in violence. This is different from the passion of wrath punished above. In a sin of wrath, it is merely the passion that is driving us. As a result, those circles had beasts that governed them, but they were simply beasts. Here there is a choice to give ourselves over to the animal nature. The result is an action that is half human, a sort of monstrosity.

15   Note the close connection between anger and violence. The minotaur is "half consumed with wrath." Interestingly, he is only *half* consumed. Anger is not the only force that drives him; he is violent, not merely wrathful.

22   We often think of the violent as particularly powerful, before whom the rest of us need to cower in fear. But here Virgil uses the minotaur's own rage against him. The minotaur's sin makes him ineffective and rather ridiculous. Dante and Virgil can easily manipulate him because he is so caught up in his anger. They know what "buttons" to push.

28   Dante's rather frightening descent down the slippery slope is an image of how we enter into sins of violence. Violence is a strange combination of passion and reason, not fully rational, but not fully unpredictable either. We get ourselves into situations in which we can expect to lose our own control. It seems to be less a matter of a clear decision than a sort of sliding down the hill we thought we would be able to walk down. We are the ones who have freely chosen to make the step, but when we place our foot on what we expect to be a solid rock, it moves beneath us.

The sliding rocks also remind us of Dante's bodiliness. These rocks don't usually move, because no one here has any weight.

40 "Every side of this deep and stinking hole shivered as if the universe felt love." The damage wasn't caused by an invading army or an overwhelming physical force. It was the result of love, which *would* turn hell on its head. Although all of hell felt the force of the earthquake, there is damage here and elsewhere, but not everywhere.

48 Here are those who use violence as a sort of strategy—what we might call "cold-blooded" violence. Tyrants are the supreme example. Here the blood they poured out on earth becomes the instrument of their own punishment. They are boiling in this river of blood, and how deeply they are submerged in it depends upon the extent of their violence.

61 The damned souls and the demons in "administration" seem to have a sort of discernment of spirits, at least in so far as they can discern sin. It is, after all, their job for all eternity. The centaurs, assigned to the ring of the violent, seem to recognize in Dante a sort of fittingness for this circle: "Which of the tortures have you come for?" (We'll see this sort of almost unspoken accusation throughout both *Inferno* and *Purgatorio*.) They don't ask what he is doing there, but *which* sin in particular is he being punished for. Before they even notice that he is still alive, they perceive in him the tendency to violence (perhaps revenge) in him. Dante, the exile, must have given himself over many times to

thoughts of revenge and maybe even to more systematic planning of violent uprising.

> VIOLENCE breaks down the rule of law. What is right or wrong ceases to count. What matters is merely who is stronger. "Might" has become "right;" now might rules. What little order that remains in society is a function of fear and intimidation. There is no appeal or argument to be made for your case. Those who rule by the power of their fists rarely understand any other sort of authority than that of force.

73 The centaurs are the enforcers of discipline here. They patrol the shores of the river of blood, making sure no one lifts himself higher than the gravity of his sin allows. Theirs is a sort of rule by force and intimidation, a hellish image of the rule the tyrants exercised on earth. The tyrants are getting a taste of their own medicine.

80 The centaur Chiron immediately notices that Dante moves things that he touches, unlike the feet of the souls of the damned. That awareness puts him on the alert, making him draw his bow.

89 "... this strange commission." Virgil treats the centaurs as they treat others. He figures force and power are all they understand. He does not explain *why* Dante is making this trip. He has been *commanded* and must obey.

CANTO 12

93   Dante needs to ride one of the centaurs in order to ford the river of blood. The centaur, who has been assigned as an enforcer in hell, is made to be a beast of burden for Dante's journey. That must be humiliating for the proud centaur. His role has shifted from a powerful enforcer who is universally feared to a beast to be ridden. He is now being *used* by Dante.

98   Dante and Virgil get Nessus assigned as their guide, the very centaur whom Virgil refused to speak with when they first met up with them, because his "will was always hot" (66). You can see Chiron using one of the standard methods of intimidation—play on the fears of your subjects, keeping them off balance. Dante and Virgil are left wondering whether there is some sort of treachery ahead. Perhaps the centaurs are so habituated in the way of thuggery that they know no other way to treat people.

Dante cannot possibly be sincere when he describes Nessus as his "trusty escort" can he? Irony seems more likely.

114   Virgil instructs Dante, "Let him speak to you first now. I will follow." The centaur has been addressing Dante directly. Is this because the centaur recognized Dante as a soul who somehow belongs here, someone with whom he was comfortable speaking? Dante, in deference to Virgil, turns to him. But here Virgil isn't the spokesman. Dante is thrust into prominence. Is this part of Virgil's plan to force Dante to face up

to his fears in general, and perhaps his own vengeful thoughts in addition?

123 "I recognized the forms of quite a few." Dante has lived through civil war. It is not surprising he would know the faces of many a sinner being punished here, perhaps numbering both from his enemies and from his allies.

CANTO 13

The Hiddenness of Human Suffering
Pain as a Cry for Help
The Self-Focus of Suffering
Treating Our Lives as Disposable
The Self-Destructiveness of Financial Irresponsibility

Much human suffering goes unobserved, and in the midst of that pain, our sense of isolation makes it worse. And what we know is true of our own suffering must also be true of the pain of others. They suffer in ways we never suspect. There might come a time when we notice a clue, a slight slip in their disguise that shocks us. The person we thought of as cheerful or "having it all together" carries an enormous burden. Then we realize that we cannot look into one another's hearts; perfect empathy never happens.

Nowhere is this brought home to us more powerfully than in the suicides of people we love. Those left behind are stricken with a double pain: we have lost people we loved, but also we wonder whether there was anything we could have done to make things different. If only we had reached out to them. . . . Why didn't they say something to us?

4 Dante does not know what he is entering. He gathers clues only gradually until he arrives at a disturbing conclusion. We will proceed step-by-step with him.

The trees here don't show signs of life at all. They are in fact images of death. Dante emphasizes this absence of life in three parallel contrasts: what few leaves remain are not green, but a dull and lifeless black; the limbs themselves are gnarled and knotted; and poisonous thorns take the place of any fruit. In each of these ways, Dante anticipates in the mind of the reader some important aspect of the sin punished here, the sin of suicide.

The black leaves are signs of the inability of the tree to support its own life; these leaves aren't producing food for the plant. There seems to be no juice flowing. They are useless appendages. In those who despair, the spark of life seems to be missing. There is no interior drive to *do* anything. It feels as though something has died.

The limbs, instead of reaching out in a healthy way, are gnarled and twisted, making an impenetrable tangle of branches. These branches call to mind a self-absorbed soul, turned in upon itself. Any new growth that *does* happen only serves to make the branches yet more tangled, more complicated, one branch interfering with its neighbor.

Trees are supposed to be not only alive but life-giving. They provide fruit to eat and branches for animals to live on. But these trees have nothing to show for being "alive." In fact, they seem to drag down everything around them. These trees, instead of sharing life, only communicate death, by means of their poisonous thorns. They don't bear "good fruit that will last" but only self-destruction.

This forest calls to mind the dark wood in which Dante found himself lost. There Dante had despaired of ever finding his way again. Here there *is* no way; not even wild animals could find a path between these knotted branches. This is, figuratively, the end of the road, a dead end. The imagery of despair and suicide are remarkably similar, and for good reason.

22 Dante hears cries again, and again cannot locate the source of the sound. He thinks someone must be hiding himself behind these hideous trees. The suffering of these souls remains hidden from his eyes.

38 The tree, a suicide, reprimands Dante for his lack of sympathy for breaking off his branch. Rather ironically, he says that Dante would treat the souls of snakes better than he treated them. After all, Dante treated them this way because he *thought* they were not even snakes, but trees, and definitely not human souls. They themselves treated their own lives with the ultimate disregard, as though they lacked human dignity,

and so here they live in the form of the lowest level of living beings, a plant.

The *passivity* of the souls here is a recurring image. As plants, they don't initiate action; things happen *to* them. They are mere recipients of actions, victims. This victimhood that they ultimately inflicted upon themselves is now immortalized in their form as trees, waiting to be broken by the actions of others.

Suicide is often portrayed as fundamentally an act of "taking control" of one's life, determining the time and manner of one's exit from that life. But here, those who have tried to gain such control, find themselves passive, at the mercy of others.

> WHEN we suffer, almost as much as we would like the pain to go away, we would like for our suffering to be understood and acknowledged. We want to be listened to. When we feel as though we have no way to express what we are going through, when we feel as though we have no voice, the isolation we feel can push us to the limits of endurance. So often, those contemplating suicide are looking not merely for an end to the suffering; they are trying to communicate to us what they are experiencing. They (and others who act in self-harming ways) are searching, in a profoundly destructive way, for their voice.

43   "So from the splintered limb came forth at once / both blood and speech." It is only when a branch has been broken and is bleeding that its voice is heard. This is a graphic image of a psychological reality about most suicides: they are trying to communicate to those around them through their suffering and death. Their death is intended to send a message—"now they'll be sorry," or "now they'll realize how much I've suffered." We've come to recognize that many *attempted* suicides are precisely this sort of attempt to communicate, a cry for help. Normal communication seems to have broken down and been replaced with this communication through the shedding of their own blood.

      In modern times, we might also consider the phenomenon of self-mutilation as belonging here. What signal is the teenager who cuts himself trying to send?

Is it an attempt to take control of some small aspect of a life that seems to be spiraling out of control? Is it a way of feeling *something* even if that something is pain? In this circle, however, the decision to break the branch is taken out of the hands of the suicides. They must wait until someone else does the breaking. Their one way of "controlling" their lives and communicating their pain has been taken away from them.

51 Does Virgil really regret telling Dante to pluck the branch? It seems to be the only way to teach Dante about the souls being punished here, and it also seems to be the only way for the souls to be able to tell their stories. There seems to be a sort of superficial respect, but it is a matter of words, merely pretending. Pretended respect for life is a recurrent theme. What respect is due to someone who willfully rejected his own life? What respect did he himself have for his own life? Who is he to ask someone to treat him better than he treated himself? The very first life we respect is our own.

> WHEN we are suffering, one of the greatest spiritual challenges is getting outside of ourselves. Stories of saints who visit and encourage other patients in the hospital while they themselves are dying of horrible diseases seem almost impossibly heroic. When we are suffering, the universe revolves around our pain. Everything else is seen through that lens. What we would normally shrug off as a minor inconvenience is viewed as an overwhelming

> burden, the last straw. Circumstances seem to conspire against us. No one understands; everyone is so inconsiderate. These are the additional burdens of the suffering souls who give in to the temptation to withdraw into themselves. They drape themselves in the mantle of victimhood, a cloak whose weight is crushing.

56 "May it not weigh you down." The canto is filled with images of burdens. To those in despair, everything seems a burden.

78 This soul blames everything around him for his final decision to take his own life, and in that, he is surely representative of most of the souls in this circle. "Envy" is the especial target for this soul, but each of the souls is a "victim" in some way. Their suicide is, in a sad irony, viewed as something that other people or circumstances did to them, or at least *drove* them to do, rather than something they chose for themselves.

84 Here Dante seems to mirror Virgil's rather ironic expression of pity. Pity is what these souls have always been searching for: it is part of their punishment that they don't receive it in hell. It can be very difficult to display any real compassion for those who make a point of complaining or who parade their suffering, but that compassion is precisely what they desire.

C. S. Lewis, a professor of medieval literature, draws on this twisted use of pity in his allegory of the afterlife *The Great Divorce*. One character, a tragic actor of the old, melodramatic school, used pity in the same way. His wife, Sarah Smith, however, won't allow it, not in heaven. "Stop it at once. . . . Using pity, other people's pity, in the wrong way. We have all done it a bit on earth, you know. Pity was meant to be a spur that drives joy to help misery. But it can be used the wrong way round. It can be used for a kind of blackmailing. Those who choose misery can hold joy up to ransom, by pity." Virgil and Dante, although keeping up polite appearances with this soul, seem to be determined not to allow pity to be used in the wrong way.

> SELF-DESTRUCTIVE acts are strangely both self-centered and profoundly disrespectful of the dignity of the self. In the misguided search to be understood as a person, the very individual we are trying to express is killed. Can there be a greater act of disrespect than treating a life as though it were a disposable and rejectable burden?

86   Virgil asks a question of the soul. He encourages the soul to answer by offering to fulfill its wish to be remembered in the living world and his memory in some way vindicated. The soul responds quite fully. But notice that never do Dante and Virgil even ask *who* this person is. How are they to remember him above and clear his name when they have no idea what that name is? This seems to be further evidence of their lack of pity. Names are curiously avoided in the canto. Their individual lives have been forfeited; they seem

to have no claim to being remembered as individuals. After all, their individuality comes from the union with their bodies.

94 "... the ferocious soul that plucks itself..." The true violence of the suicides comes through this descriptive image, even though the soul himself seems very passive and meek, giving what sounds like a "rational" explanation for his action. But the act wasn't in fact rational, but beastly—ferocious. The soul "plucks itself" from its body, like the harpies stripping leaves from the trees. The imagery is of yanking up something worthless and noxious, like a gardener pulling weeds up by the roots.

97 The souls of the suicides aren't given the dignity of even a special place in hell. They treated their lives as not worth living. Now hell treats them with the same negligent attitude. They are flung by Minos and land and are planted wherever they happen to land, like the "rankest weed." Their life is treated with *ultimate disregard*. The Harpies eat their leaves, causing them pain, and befoul them with their droppings.

103 Being treated with indignity continues at the resurrection of the body. This time, however, that lack of respect comes for the souls themselves. The bodies of the suicides will rise again, but the suicides are unique in how this resurrection happens. These souls, unlike all others in heaven and hell, according to Dante, will not be reunited with their bodies. They will never

"animate" their bodies again, for "it is not just to have what one has stripped." Their bodies are treated like burdensome objects, not as a part of the composite man. The body is referred to as "our sloughed-off skins," like a snake shedding. The souls drag their bodies through the dust, like the lazy homeowner who drags the garbage bags to the curb rather than carrying them. What difference does it make, after all? It is going to the dump anyway. Their bodies aren't *them*, just some annoying reality they tried to dispose of. The Platonic idea of the body as a prison of the soul certainly seems fitting here. Many who believed such things (dualists, we would call them) actually thought that suicide was a noble and valiant thing, a way of releasing the spiritual, immaterial soul from the bondage of matter. Bodies are disposable.

The irony is that those who perceived their bodily life as burdensome are precisely those for whom the body *becomes* a physical burden to be borne.

107 The resurrected bodies of the suicides end up hanging from the branches of their tree, impaled upon the poisonous thorns. The respective souls don't animate those bodies ever again.

We see here a sort of inversion of Christ on the cross. He willingly suffered death to make life possible for us. His sacrifice on the cross is valuable because *life* is valuable. He died on a tree, crowned with thorns, to give us new life. The suicides, on the other hand, willingly suffered death in order to escape life, not embrace it. They disposed of their lives because they saw no value in them.

Again, the image of the burdensomeness of their bodies appears. Our bodies aren't heavy when we animate them (they are just who we are), because we don't really "carry" them. If we were forced to drag them or carry them or allow them to hang from us as dead weight, our own bodies would be overwhelmingly heavy.

109 Notice that they are waiting for "the broken branch." The soul is not treated as a person. Who he was as an individual is no longer given the dignity of a name; he is merely called a broken branch. He has become identified with his suffering and seems to be nothing more.

> THE Church's social teaching has long affirmed that it is an essential part of our human dignity to be given the opportunity to manage our own material and financial resources. This teaching has led Christians to join the push for fair wages and guarantees of the right to private property. But even if society grants these fundamental rights, those who choose to waste their material goods can undermine their own ability to live with proper human dignity. Whether it is spending that is out of control or a habit of gambling, many make choices that leave them scrambling for the basic necessities of life. Those who have families drag their loved ones into the same cycle of suffering and deprivation.

115 The souls of the spendthrifts, those who have wasted their property (their livelihood), are running to escape the black dogs that are chasing them, "smashing through all the thickets in the woods." Despite the relative peacefulness of the conversation in this canto, the imagery recalls the violence of the sins punished here. The spendthrifts have been clawed and bitten by the dogs and torn to shreds by the thorny branches. Their ripping themselves on the thorns also damages the trees. They are bleeding; the trees are bleeding. Add the defilement of the Harpies and the scene is an offense to both the eyes and the nose.

127 This mad chase we have witnessed has left little bits of these sinners on the thorns and branches of the trees and even larger chunks torn away by the dogs. The spendthrifts' bodies are torn apart and scattered by the hounds, just as they scattered their property by their uncontrolled spending. We aren't talking about simple shopaholics here, who purchased in an impulsive and self-indulgent way, but people who have destroyed their lives and the lives of their families by their spending. A modern version of Dante's masterpiece would probably include those with addiction to gambling here, who wager away their income and the support they owe to their families.

132 ". . . torn in vain." On earth, the suicides decided to inflict suffering upon themselves, often as a way of communicating their distress to those around them.

Here, the suffering is taken from their hands. The Harpies and the spendthrifts are the ones who inflict it by running madly through the trees as they escape the hounds and breaking off their branches. And the suffering, which used to be at least a twisted form of communication, here is in vain—there is no one there to listen, no one who can respond with compassion. The soul of the suicide views it all as somehow unfairly targeting him. As one of the broken and bleeding trees cried out after an inconsiderate spendthrift who ran through his branches: "Is it my fault you led a wicked life?"

139 Again the soul ends up vaguely anonymous. Some details of his life are given, but no name.

CANTO 14

Destroying Our Peace of Mind
The Obsessive Call to Disbelief
The By-Products of Evil

When we are angry, and especially when we allow that anger to spill over into violence, our peace of mind is destroyed. We are now internally in a state of warfare, and this war is not merely declared against a particular enemy. We are angry at the world, angry at life in general. We look for opportunities to fight back and rebel, just as Saint Paul did before his conversion. "Saul, Saul, why do you persecute me? It hurts you to kick against the goads" (Acts 26:14). But where does it get us? When our overwhelming drive is to destroy, we are left with nothing but barren ground as our reward.

1   Out of compassion for his countryman, Dante (like a gardener collecting clippings for disposal) gathers the broken branches of the suicide. He can't give the

branches back to him any more than the suicide can take back his life. All Dante can do is lay them at the foot of the tree. What good can they do the tree now?

6   Dante describes the scene displayed before him as a "fearful work of justice." Dante is increasingly recognizing the justice of what he sees. Is that because he is growing in an awareness of the true disorder of sin or because these are sins that affect him less personally?

9   This desert is so barren that it seems actively to reject anything that attempts to grow there: "refusing every plant." The only "life" we see are the trees of the suicides that ring this desert. Barrenness is the dominant image here in this third round of the seventh circle, and for good reason. This barrenness will stand as a symbol for a surprising collection of sins, and it arises from the devastating destructiveness of violence.

16 Some sort of conversion of heart seems to be occurring in Dante, that change that begins with attrition, that imperfect sorrow for our sins that is rooted in fear of punishment. "The fear of the Lord is the beginning of wisdom." It might not be the height of wisdom; it isn't where we want to end up. But it *is* a start. We hope to move beyond the fear of punishment as our motivation; we want to do what is right out of love, love of God in particular. We want to move from attrition (imperfect contrition) to perfect contrition that is powered by love.

22   We see in this part of the round a variety of punishments, corresponding to the various ways in which these souls were violent against God. These souls are identified by their respective postures on the burning sand: some of them run, some sit, and others lie on their backs, facing the burning flakes head-on. The largest of these groups was those who ran. These souls seem to be those who rejected God's gift of the fertility of their sexuality. Perhaps their running means that they are so focused upon their sexual activity that they don't really pay attention to God; it is not that they reject him consciously, but that they run about their sexual "business," without any thought of God or of religion.

Those who sit, without any apparent activity except working for their own sustenance (eating and brushing away the burning flakes) are the usurers, whom we shall see more of in canto 17.

Those who lay face up are fewer but more vocal. These seem to be blasphemers. In their own way, they were obsessed with God; they ranted and raved at him and seem to have made a sort of vocation out of being unbelievers. In a strange way, the God they rejected became the focus of their lives. The modern world provides us with numerous examples of this twisted sort of "divinity obsession," people who write books and go on talk shows to convince everyone that they are foolish to believe in God. Some religious people spend less time actively discussing theological issues than do these "professional atheists." Not surprisingly, they endure their punishment with their faces lifted to God, not in praise or adoration, but in defiance and blasphemy.

28 The imagery here is particularly jarring. If you simply leave out the word *fire*, the tone is pastoral and peaceful, like snow falling on a windless day in the Alps. But the cooling and nourishing snow that the imagery suggests is here replaced by flakes of fire. Precipitation is supposed to water the earth and make it fertile; here the precipitation comes in the form of fire, destroying rather than nourishing, making barren rather than fertile. God's word is intended to fall upon us like refreshing dew. These souls have rejected that revealed word and the spiritual fertility it is supposed to bring. God is the vine and we are the branches. Without him, we wither and die.

Scripture is filled with the general idea of the fruitfulness of divine truth and grace. But the precise imagery Dante uses here also has clear scriptural associations. The punishment of Sodom and Gomorrah comes immediately to mind, with its fire and brimstone. In the nineteenth chapter of Genesis, we saw unnatural sexual acts being punished but also the blasphemy directed towards God himself. The land was rendered infertile by being strewn with salt.

In addition, in Revelation, chapter 16, seven angels pour out seven bowls of wrath. The fourth of these bowls was fiery and led to blasphemy: "The fourth angel poured his bowl on the sun, and it was allowed to scorch men with fire; men were scorched by the fierce heat, and they cursed the name of God who had power over these plagues, and they did not repent and give him glory." Blasphemy and punishment by fire belong together.

37 The fire burns in a double way: when it lands on the souls punished here (making them have to constantly be brushing the flakes constantly from their skin) and when it ignites the sand on which it lands. The sand is burning sand not just because it is burning hot, as is the case in our earthly experience; it is literally burning because it is flammable. Those flakes the souls somehow manage to avoid end up burning them anyway when they ignite the sand around them

39 "Without / a moment's pause." Everything in this world should have served as a reminder of the God who created it. Every human being should be mindful of God. We are intended, even by reason alone, to be led from the visible things of creation to the invisible God who created them (see Rom 1:19–20; Ws 13). Most of us live lives of almost total unawareness of the divine splendor hidden in creation. We just do not notice. The souls here are forced to live in a constant state of awareness, not because the truth can lead them to God (the time for that has passed), but because each flake burns them to alertness.

> MUCH of the world we live in is not hostile to religion or to God. It is merely indifferent. Religion is as irrelevant as outdated technology. We forget about it; it just does not even appear on our radar. But there are others (and they are overrepresented in the media) who seem to make their careers out of fighting against God and all he teaches. He is a constant presence in their minds. They are obsessed with him because he is the target of their anger and their violent reactions.

51 This soul appears almost heroic. He lets the flakes fall upon him without brushing them away. He seems almost stoical about the pain. Perhaps he sees reacting to the pain as an acknowledgment of the reality of God and his punishments. But, in addition to his heroic endurance, we immediately perceive the hardness of heart of this soul: "What I was living, so am I still, dead!" Even in hell, he still curses God, rather than acknowledging his own wrongdoing.

63 Virgil rightly remarks that Capaneus's very raging is his punishment. Even here, the focus of his life is God, the God he rejects and even hates. What is more painful than to be obsessed with the object of our hate? God infuriates him, but he cannot turn away.

72 ". . . the fittest decorations for his chest." Capaneus was a military man, but instead of military ribbons and decorations, he wears the scars from the burning flakes of fire. They are a fitting tribute to the battle he

fought in life and the battle he continues to fight even here in hell, a battle he poured his strength into and sacrificed his life for: the battle against God.

76 We come across the river of blood in which the tyrants were punished. Here it runs across the desert before it falls over the cliff into the pit of fraud. This river running through the burning sand also reminds us of the connection of these less obviously "violent" sins with the ones that came before. Although the sins of the tyrants were more dramatic and bloodier, these through which we are now passing are more serious morally, punished deeper in the pit of hell. The sins of the physically violent were more often driven in part by passion. The violence against God we see punished here is a clearly chosen position or lifestyle.

82 The river has raised stone embankments on either side. Usually we see such embankments to keep the river from overflowing its banks and to protect the surrounding land. Here this "protection" is taken to extremes. We would normally expect to see signs of life around a river running through a desert, but the embankments contain the river, keeping it from even moistening the burning sand. Here there is to be no leafy oasis: just barrenness.

88 It is a strange thing that a river of boiling blood somehow "cools and quenches" the burning flakes. Various interpreters have assigned meanings to the fact that the fiery snow doesn't fall over this river. I'm not sure

whether any of these interpretations rings obviously true, or whether this is merely a literary device to get Virgil and Dante across the burning sands.

94   The "mountain lush with leaf and spring" has become barren, like the landscape before Dante and Virgil.

> THE one crop that never seems to run short in this fallen world of ours is the harvest of tears, suffering, and strife that we sow so abundantly. But what do we do with this enormous stockpile of evil, like radioactive waste infecting and contaminating all that comes near it? Our world can feel like a moral sewer at times. But where does it drain?

103   Virgil uses the myth of the Old Man of Crete (which also appears in the Old Testament) to explain the source of the rivers of hell. We can see the rivers as a sort of "runoff" of all the sufferings, tears, and blood from the world above. It comes "guttering down from our world above." They are a sort of sewage of suffering and evil. What appears to be four different rivers (Acheron, Styx, Phlegethon, and Cocytus) is in fact merely one river encountered on different levels of hell. We saw Acheron when we saw the souls being ferried into hell proper. Styx was where those souls suffering from wrath and sloth were punished in the muddy marsh. Phlegethon is the bloody and boiling river in which the violent are punished. Cocytus is yet to come: the frozen river in the very pit of hell.

136 The final of the traditional classical rivers of the underworld, Lethe, however, is missing. Virgil wants us to know that this is more than just an oversight. Lethe exists, but it is not here. Lethe is the river of forgetfulness. The souls in hell are not to be given the luxury of forgetting. Remembering the past is all they have, since they have rejected the "eternal present" which is God. Only the repentant souls in purgatory, at the end of their purification, are granted this gift of forgetfulness, laying aside all regret and feelings of guilt so that they can enter into God's presence, the eternal "now," without the past being a burden. How good that sounds. The souls in hell are sentenced to a life as prisoners of the past.

CANTO 15

The Holiness of Sexuality
Silence in the Face of Wrong
Sin and Cover-Up

It is at least ironic that our sex-obsessed world accuses Christianity of being fixated upon matters of sexual morality. Somehow they argue that the Church still looks at sex in a dualistic sort of way, rejecting it as something sordid and bodily. We cannot deny that two of the Ten Commandments are about sexual matters, but the reason for this divine emphasis is not because sex is something dirty but because it is something holy. In paradise, God commanded Adam and Eve to go forth and multiply, and that meant sex. For Christians, sexuality is an act that not only gives pleasure but also allows us to cooperate with the creative act of God in the production of a new human being with an immortal soul. In his wisdom, God united the pleasure of sexual activity with the possibility of new life. What God has joined, let no man put asunder.

16   We now meet those sinners who run across the burning sand, sinners who are much more numerous than the blasphemers. Modern people might be surprised by Dante's treatment of this sin, or even that it *should* be considered a sin. Some others might be taken aback by the number of those who have sinned against God by sinning against the sexual nature he has created. For Dante, our sexuality is a gift from God to be respected. We *are* given dominion over it, but that dominion requires us to respect the nature we have been given. Dominion is not a veto power over nature, or permission to remake it according to our desires. Dominion calls us to recognize the nature God has created and to work in accordance with that nature. Our calling, entrusted to us by God himself, is to bring that nature to its fulfillment, not to alter the nature itself.

> HUMAN beings are noted for their ability to communicate. The development of language is one of the marks of our rationality. But often we are just as eloquent in what we choose not to say. For one reason or another, we often choose to avert our eyes and keep our mouths shut. But as Saint Thomas More famously said in his trial, "Qui tacit, consentit." He who remains silent, consents.

18   Dante is met by the stares of the next group of sinners in this ring. He goes, rather uncomfortably, from being the observer to being the observed. Next, he is grabbed by his tunic's hem. Knowing the sin that

CANTO 15

is punished here, these images set an odd tone, one which is vaguely disturbing without any concrete evidence pointing to something obviously inappropriate. This seems fitting given that homosexuality (one of the sins punished here), especially in Dante's time when the action was considered not only sinful but also illegal, worked by way of suggestion and hint.

This canto is marked by a clear division between what is happening on the surface and what is being suggested beneath that surface, between what is being offered for public consumption and the reality beneath. In the canto itself, while Dante and Virgil are walking and conversing with the souls here, the sin goes unmentioned and unnamed, as though it were a sort of "open secret," known but unacknowledged.

30 ". . . are *you* here?" Dante seems to be surprised that his former teacher Brunetto Latini is punished here. Latini was a trusted and valued teacher, a sort of role model for the young Dante. Perhaps Dante was previously unaware of Latini's sin; is he shocked by *what* Latini is punished for, or by the *fact* that he ended up getting punished for it?

31 ". . . my son." These words take on a different atmosphere when we recognize that this sin often works by abusing positions of trust and authority. In the ancient world and in the Middle Ages, the sin of homosexuality was most often between older men and youths; it often seemed as much a sort of worship of youth

as something purely sexual. One suspects, given the horrifying revelations concerning the abuse scandal involving priests and bishops as well as other authority figures, that not much has changed. The trust given to someone people call "Father" is betrayed. Whether that fatherhood is biological, intellectual, or spiritual, using it to obtain sexual pleasure is a kind of incest.

34   Dante seems eager to spend time with Latini: "I beg you, please, with all my heart." When they begin to walk together, Dante "bowed my head as one who, walking, shows his reverence." Is this a sign of respect for his position, a mark of personal affection, or indifference to the sin he committed?

37   The burning "snowflakes" are still the punishment, as

they were for the blasphemers, but the significance has shifted slightly. With the blasphemers, the emphasis was on the love of God, which either warms or burns depending upon one's receptivity, and is supposed to produce fruit in the hearts of believers. For them, God's grace was rendered barren, and his supernatural fruitfulness was rejected.

Here with the sodomites, the attention turns to a more natural sort of love: human sexual love. That, too, is supposed to be a sign of love and to be fruitful. But sins of unnatural sexual activity destroy both the unitive and procreative aspects of sexual love. What was intended by God to be a sign of loving bond between the spouses and a source of fruitfulness has become casual and barren sex, devoid of both life and love. Modern readers might consider whether other sins against the fruitfulness of sex should be included here. What would Dante do with unnatural sins between men and women (sodomy or oral sex) or artificial contraception? Sins against the nature of sexuality are certainly a much broader category than the category of homosexuality.

The sinners here are sentenced to an eternal restlessness. Their punishment is to bear the heat of the burning flakes while running incessantly. Perhaps this is because when sexuality is disconnected with its natural end, it can never relax. There is always another conquest to be made, more pleasure to be pursued. When sexuality has no purpose except that which we give to it, there is little to hold us back from promiscuity. It is like eating food for its taste, even though that food does not nourish and therefore cannot satisfy.

55   Latini's words sound subtly flattering: "Follow your star and you will never fail to find your glorious port." Combined with his claim that he personally would have guided Dante, if only he hadn't died when Dante was young, his words seem to suggest he is insinuating himself into Dante's life, a sort of subtle seduction. Is this discussion an expression of the teacher-student relationship they had on earth, or a sort of glimpse into the way this sin works? How, after all, could Latini "have given you strength to do your work"?

79   Dante seems to have fallen for Latini's manipulation—he sees no justice in his being in hell. "If I could have my wishes heard in full, . . . you would not even now be banished from our life." How does this fit with Dante's purpose here? Isn't he supposed to be witnessing the natural and just consequences of sinfulness? Dante refers to Latini as being "like a father," but it is that very fatherly relationship which he has abused and violated. Why is it here, of all places, that the justice of the punishment goes unremarked? One might even expect Virgil to intervene, "Remember why we are here: not to socialize with the sinners punished here, but to understand the justice of God's ways and to turn ourselves from the ways of sin."

86   Dante recognizes that much that Ser Brunetto had done was beneficial to those around him. He remains

grateful and promises to fulfill that debt of gratitude by his words. Is this another manifestation of the difference between the outward life and the inward sin?

95 Dante seems to be more detached from the ups and downs of life, ready for whatever fortune throws his way. Virgil seems pleased by Dante's progress and compliments him for his comments.

> SOME sins seem to produce a sort of united front against disclosure to the world, a sort of code of silence. Organized crime would be impossible without this commitment to silence. No matter what, you do not spill the beans. Sexual abuse by persons in positions of authority is, unfortunately, another example of closed ranks of silence. Is it scandalous to speak about such things or more scandalous to keep quiet?

100 When Dante asks Ser Brunetto about the "worthiest and the most famous of his company," Latini's flow of words dries up: "To know of some is well; it merits praise to pass the rest in silence." Why does silence merit praise? The culture of secrecy and silence continues among these souls, even in hell. Cover-up is still their modus operandi. Language isn't used truly to communicate, but in order to draw others in. All we are told is that the sinners (the character of their sin is still technically undisclosed) are from the highest ranks of teachers and clerics, the most scandalous

of whom are revealed, perhaps because their sin was already clearly public knowledge.

112 Here we are presented with a sinning bishop, transferred from one see to another, even though his sin was known by those in authority. How sadly similar to scandals in our own day.

118 "People approach with whom I must not be." Perhaps Brunetto isn't permitted to mix freely, but must stay with his own group. There is almost a note of danger and menace here.

121 The reference to stripping for athletic contest also subtly calls back to mind the nature of the sin.

CANTO 16

A Culture of Secrecy
Public Honor and Private Shame

Secrecy requires effort. Keeping something secret requires organization, cooperation, and planning. As a result, secret sins naturally tend to spill over into systematic fraud. They put us on the edge of something far more dangerous and corrupt.

1   From here, while still walking among the sodomites, Dante and Virgil can already hear the sound of the waterfall crashing into the pit of fraud. That auditory cue is Dante's way of implanting the idea of fraud while we are looking at these next sins. The echo of fraud is in the background. These sinners use their powers of reason and persuasion to achieve their goals, and that is the beginning of fraud.

10 A soul calls out to Dante that he should stop and speak with him. His horrible wounds and scars from past

burns are shocking. Are these suggestive of the terrible sores of venereal diseases? Dante and people of his time would be familiar with the physical effects of sexual promiscuity by witnessing the horrible symptoms of untreated sexually transmitted diseases.

14 Virgil seems to be encouraging Dante to respect the souls he finds here. "One should be courteous to men like these." Dante should be the one humbling himself by approaching them, rather than making them approach him. These men were politicians and warriors, people who have given great service to their countries, even more than the scholars and clerics we've already met.

Virgil reminds Dante to recognize their contribution to society as something real, regardless of their sins. Their actions are still worthy of our gratitude. Again we see the distinction in this circle between the outward life of valor that makes them worthy of enduring respect and the inward or hidden life of sin that merited their place in this circle. Perhaps their contributions *actually* make their present state even sadder, for how the great have fallen.

22 The imagery of oiled, naked athletes locked together like wrestlers hints at both the physical prowess of these men of action but also their sin. And what should we make of the description of them "warily searching where and when to seize / their chance"? If the punishment here, as elsewhere, is a sort of embodiment of the

sin itself, we get some suggestion of the deceptiveness of this sin, so close to the edge of fraud.

28   Here we get an acknowledgment that this sin is particularly subject to scorn. The souls assume that Dante feels that scorn, and ask him, because of their earthly reputations, to speak to them and tell them his name.

44   Rusticucci seems to blame his "shrewish wife." He is a married man who somehow violated the sanctity of the married state. We know nothing about his wife, but it is tempting to think that she took some sort of cruel revenge upon him when his sins were discovered. Women married to sexually promiscuous men ran the grave risk of contracting terrible diseases merely by having sexual relations with their infected husbands. She had multiple reasons for being "upset."

> In North America, we expect our public figures to be not only capable of governing but also outstanding in their personal and moral lives. We expect them to be not only leaders but also role models. When we discover personal hypocrisies in which they do not live in accordance with their stated principles, or moral failures in which they fail to live up to the standard we expect from great people, we judge them to be less fit for public service. The juxtaposition of the public honor and the private shame is particularly painful. Seeing both their talent and their failure is a cause of sadness, sadness for greatness wasted, for honor tarnished.

46 Dante professes his willingness to "cast myself among them." We've seen before that when Dante experiences pity for the souls he meets, or feels what he erroneously perceives to be the injustice of what they suffer, he himself is often in need of purging from that particular sin. Is his willingness to walk with these men on the burning sand another example of a subtle confession of his own sins, or merely a sign of human respect for the service they provided to society in the world? Many were patriots who fought on what Dante would have thought was the "right side" of his civil war. The "good will that made me crave to clasp within my arms the three down there" is certainly a vivid image. His assurance to these souls that what he feels is "sorrow, not loathing" might seem to be another example of Dante sympathizing with these souls in a way similar to what he felt for Paolo and Francesca in the circle of the lustful.

But perhaps this case is different. If Dante were not understanding the justice of the punishment, if he were falling again into a sort of misplaced sympathy for those in hell, would not Virgil, his trustworthy guide, have intervened? Perhaps the honor Dante gives to these men is in fact part of the punishment, only sharpening the sense of that loss.[3]

67 These men of public affairs are eager for news of their homeland. Their lack of knowledge of the present, of

---

[3] See Esolen's note on canto 15, line 30, on this same sort of sadness concerning Ser Brunetto.

"current affairs," is particularly difficult for men who are accustomed to being "in the know."

85 The language is again very gentle, so much so that it is easy to forget we are in a circle punishing violence, violence against nature. The souls "fled on feet as swift / as slender wings. One could not say 'amen' as quickly as the three had disappeared." Their leaving has an almost angelic sound to it. Appearances and reality again are at odds with each other.

106 The rope Dante wears around his waist sounds like the knotted cord often worn by religious or members of religious Third Orders as a sign of dedication to chastity. A similar sort of idea is still contained in the vesting prayers for the priest when he puts on his cincture before Mass, asking for the gifts of self-control and chastity. This idea is given further weight by the fact Dante thought of trying to snare the leopard, the symbol of lust, with that same cord. Here, after the rather confusing imagery of the ring of the sodomites, Virgil asks him to remove that cord. Without any explanation, he throws it off the cliff. The cord, like the light signals at the gates of the city of Dis, seems to be a way of summoning their transport to the next level. Perhaps the cord, also signifying something like obedience, is the only way to be able to keep one's bearings in the territory of fraud.

115 Even Dante recognizes that Virgil's action in throwing the cord was strange: "Some strange new thing must

correspond / to the strange gesture my good Teacher makes."

118 The imagery here, by which Dante intends to prepare us for what is to come, is of being able to see beneath the confusing or deceptive surface and understand the truth hidden below. If Virgil can truly see in this way, he is an appropriate guide through the treacherous rings of the fraudulent.

124 ". . . whose face appears a lie." Again Dante anticipates the next subject with his imagery. In the area in which sins of fraud are punished, nothing quite is what it appears to be. Fraud puts forward a false face or façade, behind which lurks an ugly and dangerous reality. The figure Dante sees swimming up from the abyss is the personification of that disparity between the face presented to the public and the reality behind it.

CANTO 17

Fraud and Isolation
Work as an Element of Human Perfection
Trusting as We Step Into the Unknown

Many works of fiction begin with the premise of nothing being really as it seems. Whether they are stories of espionage and counterespionage, conspiracy theories, or science fiction like *The Matrix*, the characters struggle to tell what way is up and whom they can trust. How do we function in a world when our perceptions and the underlying reality do not seem to correspond? Every action is fraught with complications.

We do not need to enter a parallel universe to experience this dizzying confusion, because such is the world of fraud. How do we communicate with liars? How do we connect with traitors? Fraud turns the world into an isolated chaos, in which it is every man for himself.

10   Geryon is the very picture of fraud: the face of an

honest man united with the body of a serpent, and offspring of the "Father of Lies." His "paws were furry to the shoulder tops," displaying to us his willingness to use brute force, if necessary, to attain his ends. The swirls of colors decorating his body (aside from the association with Islam, which Dante subtly includes) are probably intended as a sort of distraction, almost dizzying in complexity, like the scheming of the fraudulent man or the misdirection of the close-up magician. They might also serve as a sort of camouflage, like the markings on a snake's skin, allowing him to blend into his surroundings unnoticed.

22 The predatory beaver is a bizarre and unexpected image. But the point of the imagery is clear: Geryon has his belly on the edge of the cliff (like beer-drinking Germans leaning on the bar!), hiding his dangerous parts out of view. If Dante and Virgil weren't some distance away, they would never have witnessed anything but the kindly face of the beast. Hanging off the edge is a venomous tail. What you see is definitely *not* what you get. What is presented or promised (the honest face) is merely a front for the evil scheming of the fraudulent man (the sting at the end of the tail). This dichotomy between what is apparent and what is under the surface will be a recurrent theme for all of the cantos on fraud, in fact, for the rest of the *Inferno*.

28 Having come to the end of the stream's bank at the waterfall where the river pours into the pit of the

fraudulent, Virgil and Dante walk along the cliff's edge, obviously protected from the burning sands by the stony verge. In order to approach Geryon (and Virgil has yet to explain to Dante why anyone would want to do that), they'll travel along the edge, meeting that final group of sinners in this circle, the usurers.

41   Again, before we are told who these sinners are, Dante prepares our minds with his imagery. Virgil goes to "haggle" with the beast, anticipating the financial misdeeds of the souls Dante goes off to meet. Again, even before we are officially informed who these sinners are, the imagery has already given us a clue.

Note that Geryon, the symbol of fraud, is going to be their means of transport to the bottom of the cliff. The fraudulent make a career of manipulating others for their own ends. Here Geryon is the one being used, and for God's end. In hell, the professional users get used.

44   How often is Dante not only allowed, but even commanded, to go off on his own, without the guidance and protection of Virgil? But here that is what happens. What is the significance of that? Perhaps it has something to do with Dante's own financial struggles after all his property was confiscated at the time of his exile from Florence. Has he had bitter dealings with money-lenders before? This is something Virgil wants him to face alone.

46   The tone of pity for their "sorrowing streams" of tears

is quickly pushed aside by the comparison with flee-bitten dogs, scratching and biting themselves. Whatever pity Dante felt for those he knew among the sodomites is noticeably lacking here.

> WE were intended in the Garden of Eden to work; it is part of our perfection and dignity. Adam was given the task of tending the garden when he was still in paradise. Work was part of his blessedness not a punishment. Original sin is not the reason we have to work: it merely made our work toilsome rather than personally rewarding. Our work is intended to be a sort of personal expression. We place our mark on the world by what we do or make. What we *are* inside is expressed by what we *do* outside. Our Lord worked with Saint Joseph at Nazareth. Work is holy; work helps us to be fully who we are intended to be.

52 The faces here are unrecognizable. It is as though their sin has sapped their humanity. How often have debtors wondered whether their lenders had a human heart—symbolically Dante answers the question negatively: they aren't allowed a human identity. In modern terms, we see how businessmen often hide their cruel decisions behind "company policy."

This lack of individual identity might also have a deeper source. As we shall see, these men have rejected the human labor that would have completed their humanity. These souls, by lacking their proper labor, lack their own distinct individuality.

55   Here the only mark of identification is their family seal, a sort of corporate logo. These were "company men," through and through. Dante will later specify the various families in Florence who were stained by this sin. Everyone would recognize them by their coats of arms. The sinners have these family money bags slung around their necks, like horses with their feedbags. Like gluttons staring at their food, each usurer "seemed to gorge his eyes upon that feast." Rather than exerting themselves, making something of themselves, they fed themselves off of the wealth of their families and off of other people's labor. Their passivity is not something upper class. It makes them beastly rather than fully human.

67   A proud member of the Scrovegni family tells Dante, "Get lost." Despite their lack of any personal accomplishment, despite the obvious fact that they are condemned to hell, these souls are contemptuous in their treatment of Dante. They have always viewed other persons as merely means to an end, an opportunity for profit. They acknowledge neither their own dignity nor that of others.

73   This soul from one of the "good" families of Padua shows himself to be anything but noble. His sin has made him beastly—sticking out his tongue like an ox. We have already seen them compared to flea-bitten

dogs. Their beastliness is a sign of the violence they have shown to their own nature, their humanity. These souls are violent against human nature, which is supposed to sustain itself (make a profit) by using its own talents, by its own labor. The parable of the talents shows us what God expects of us. We've been given talents in order to make use of them. Turning money into a means of making more money denies the necessity and value of human industry. Look back at the discussion of the nature of usury when Virgil was explaining the organization of hell to Dante in canto 11 (11:94 to the end). Human industry is called the "grandchild of God." God is the maker of all things, pure actuality. We, made in his image, his children, are called to imitate him in his activity. Our work is intended to be *our* child, and hence, God's grandchild. We are fruitless if we do not produce something by our labor.

We should mention that Dante seems to be stricter than Saint Thomas about whether any lending of money at interest was usury. Thomas recognizes that lending involves risk, and that risk should be compensated. But to take advantage of another's need in order to charge as much as one can get away with is clearly usury. I'd be tempted to put some owners of places specializing in payday loans and perhaps even some big banks with their credit cards here too.

> TRUSTING in God each moment of our lives and cooperating with the graces he sends us can lead us to places we never intended to visit. Once we start listening to God in our hearts, he keeps moving us further and further from what we find comfortable. Saint John Paul II gave the text "Duc in altum" (Lk 5:4) as a motto for World Youth Day in Toronto in 2002. "Put out into the deep," push away from the familiar shore without fear of what lies ahead, confident that God will provide for your needs abundantly.

79   Dante now realizes that he is going to have to *ride* Geryon. Virgil is already mounted, waiting for him to finish his discussion. Again, Dante is reminded of the need for courage. "Be fearless now and strong."

85   Dante is shaking in his boots with fear; it is only the fact that Virgil is between him and that venomous tail and the thought of the shame he would feel in Virgil's presence if he tried to back out that make him obey. Even then, when Dante tries to ask Virgil to hold him tight, his voice just won't come out. Virgil, however, knows his need for encouragement and provides it, without Dante having to put his humiliating neediness into words. It's a lovely picture of how God provides for our needs, even when we are unable to give voice to them.

100   Imagine the natural fear rising up within Dante. He is on the back of the monstrous Geryon. This beast has just

pushed himself off the cliff. Dante must have felt what a first-time passenger feels when his plane takes off.

112 Dante can see nothing all around him. The pit into which he is descending is in darkness. The only way he knows he is even descending is by the feeling of the air blowing against his face. The image is one of absolute trust. He is entering a dark pit. Virgil is holding on to him, and that is all he needs to know. For the Christian, our awareness of God's presence and his providence should provide the same consolation and confidence.

CANTO 18

Self-Defensiveness in a Harsh World
Sex And Deception
Using Sex as a Means of Manipulation
Flattery, a Costly Exchange

Fraud or dishonesty in all its forms breaks down our connection with one another in our families and in society as a whole. We learn from painful experience that we cannot trust others; we view them as competitors, adversaries, even enemies. This awareness produces in us a self-defensiveness that in turn leads us to isolate ourselves increasingly from one another. We end up surrounded by people, but somehow very alone. But to the eyes of those affected by fraud, that sadly is the way things appear. Both those who practice fraud and those who are on the receiving end of it develop a bunker mentality.

1   Immediately upon arriving in the pit of fraud, we recognize that even the terrain is different here from

what we have encountered in the upper levels of hell. The circles of the passionate and the violent were flat terraces. Here, where fraud is punished, there are ten Malebolge—literally, evil pockets or pouches. These Malebolge are stone trenches that run all the way around its circle, like the dug-in trenches famous in the First World War. Together, these trenches form a series of concentric rings around the central (and final) pit of hell.

There seems at least two different ways to think about this shift in the geographical imagery. The first interpretation follows from the nature of the sin of fraud. Since fraud is based upon a sort of deception, a false face, it takes place underground, underhandedly, covertly, out-of-sight. They have thrived in hiding.

Second, we can think of the Malebolge in their relation to Satan himself. In the same way that a medieval city had outer walls protecting the gardens, inner walls protecting the houses, and a moat and walls protecting the citadel or stronghold, Satan's city—the opposite of the City of God in heaven—has the outer gates (broken and off their hinges after Our Lord's death), the city walls of the city of Dis, and now these moats leading to the deepest pit of hell. The Malebolge are Satan's inner defenses—his moats manned by his most faithful troops, the followers of the Father of Lies (see lines 10–11).

The iron colored stone suggests the coldness of heart of the fraudulent—"I will take from your flesh the heart of stone" (Ez 36:26). Their sins were not driven by their passions. They did evil in a cold-blooded way.

14 There are small stone bridges ("rock-ribs") running over the Malebolge that will allow Virgil and Dante to pass over these trenches on their journey to the bottom.

> IN his poem *Marmion*, Sir Walter Scott wrote the immortal words: "O, what a tangled web we weave when first we practice to deceive!" Sinful human beings will use almost any sticky material to construct their web, whatever will attract and hold their prey. From the beginning of recorded history, we have exploited sexuality as a ploy for achieving other hidden ends. Our sexuality is at the very core of our humanity; it is a powerful drive, one that is easily manipulated.

25 Interestingly, the souls in hell are sometimes specifically identified as nude, as they are here. I don't suppose the others actually have clothing (Dante explains the appearance of bodies and even clothing in the *Purgatorio*, canto 25), but they appear naked here as a symbol of their sins: pandering and seducing; that is, leading people into sexual sins either with others (pandering or pimping) or with oneself (seducing), both of which actions are types of fraud. These related sins account for the two-way traffic in the trench.

35 The devils have horns (often a symbol of lust) and are

whipping the sinners with thick whips, as they themselves used their reason to drive others into sexual sins. Here the sinners are on the receiving end. Notice an interesting shift. Sometimes the sin itself is the punishment (the suicides are good examples of this) and sometimes the sin which the sinner inflicted upon others is turned upon himself (a taste of his own medicine). These sinners used the sexual desires of others to entice them into sin, driving them on, manipulating them with the whip of desire. That desire, the most powerful in our human nature, usually receives a swift response, just like the souls here who respond immediately to the "first strokes" of the whip. In so many cases, repeated temptation is not necessary. The very first one receives its response from our disordered nature.

46   Notice how the soul tries to hide. Hiding is part of fraud, and being exposed means failure. It is only "against my will I'll tell." Dante reminds us of the very core of fraud when he says, "If your face and its features aren't false . . ." The man should hide, given that he used his own sister to lead someone to sin sexually. Being recognized by Dante (the equivalent of being pulled out of a line-up) is certainly part of his punishment.

> USING sexuality as a means of getting what we want is a very different sin from lust. The lustful soul desires the pleasure of the sexual act, but the one who exploits

> sexuality is looking for something else. The sex is merely the bait. This sort of manipulation is not a function of human weakness but of calculating wickedness. The real object of desire is what sex will bring them: money, power, or status.

63   Venedico reveals the underlying motivation of his pandering: avarice. He was merely *using* sex as a means to attain wealth.

65   The horsewhipping demon won't let the souls talk their way out of anything or pretend to be something they aren't: "Off with you, pimp! We're no whores for you to swindle here." Again, exposure is part of their punishment. There is nothing that was hidden that will not be exposed. In hell, the subterfuges of the fraudulent are dragged into the light of day. Deception or hiding the truth is not permitted.

70   It is from the arch of these bridges, or preferably from the far side of the Malebolge, which is significantly lower, that Dante observes the sinners. Until now, Dante and Virgil have been walking in one direction and so have seen the faces of only one half of this two-way procession of sinners: the panderers. As they get atop the bridge, they look in the other direction and see the parade of seducers, moving briskly along, also driven by the whips of the demons.

85   We should not think that the seducers are merely prostitutes and courtesans. These are certainly included.

This circle punishes all of those who have used sex as a tool. Among those would be many men who have "loved them and left them," have promised love for sex only to renege on the promise once they have what they want. Jason is one of those.

97 "Seducers go with him, all liars. That's enough for you to know of this first ditch." There is no romanticizing of the sin of seduction. This is not a matter of love in excess, or even of sexual desire in excess, as was the case with Paolo and Francesca in the circle of the lustful. That is wrong, but understandable given the weakness of our human nature. This sin is about lying in order to get what is desired. The "lie" of seduction is not merely the words that are used to convince the victim to commit sexual sin (that *can* be part of it, but not all of it), but the very act of sex itself. Sex is supposed to be a sign of commitment to one's spouse, a way of communicating an exclusive and inseparable bond. The truth of sexual relationship is violated here. The sex itself becomes a lie—an idea that the modern world would, unfortunately, barely understand. What is being presented as the "false face" here is the bond of love, but casual sex for the sake of money or influence is the ugly reality behind that face.

> HUMAN language is seen by many scholars as a special sign of our developed rationality. Words provide us a way of communicating with one another, of sharing the truth I have in my mind with someone else. The

> wonderfully powerful tool of language makes society possible; it also opens the possibility for literature. But our words can be used as deceptive bait too. We can abuse this precious gift and use it as a way to get what we want. Some people have a gift for saying the "right thing" to win over others, whether what they say is true or not. Flattery has become a lucrative art form, but at what cost to our human dignity?

103 From what we can *see* of the people in the next malebolgia, we can conclude that they are in a sad state and seem to lack any sort of self-respect. "We came upon people who whimpered, sniveling, runny-nosed, who slapped and smacked themselves with open palms." They seem like the poorest of the poor—unhealthy, whining, hitting themselves like a crazy street person. Any sense of dignity has been lost long ago.

106 Their surroundings match their personal state. They are in the bottom of what could best be described as a latrine, growing with fungus and mold, like a toilet which hasn't been cleaned in decades, and sending off a smell, "making a nauseous brawl with eyes and nose." It's hard to tell whether the sight or the smell was worse.

112 The toilet imagery immediately becomes more obvious: "I saw people plunged deep in just the sort of dung you dump from human privies and latrines." The reason for the mold, fungus, and noxious odor

is now obvious: these souls are wallowing in excrement. In life, these flatterers were masters of BS, and now they swim in it. Their own sense of dignity didn't hold them back from saying whatever would please the rich and famous, making sure they were allowed to remain in their exalted presences. They were courtiers, frequenting palaces, and now their surroundings have changed—or perhaps the reality of their lives has merely been revealed.

Here human conversation (speaking the truth) and the social bonds of affection and loyalty are the false face that fraud offers to the world, with ambition and greed the ugly reality hidden behind.

133 Thaïs is in the second trench because, even though she was a prostitute, she also flattered her "lover," praising his sexual abilities.

Why is her flattery worse than her seducing? The words of truth are more fundamental than pledges of love. We are right to be suspicious if someone offers that sort of commitment; such a bond requires special discernment. We should, however, be able to trust the word of those around us. Without that, society becomes unsocial, because truthful communication is the foundation of our social nature. Remember, Dante's criterion for ordering these sins is how profoundly they deform our humanity, not how much external damage they do.

CANTO 19

Selling What Is Priceless
Respect and Love for a Defective Church

The online auction site eBay has had to impose restrictions on what can be listed for auction. It seems that people were offering for sale things (or actions) that, even by the norms of secular society, were considered unacceptable. Is there anything that someone would not sell? Is nothing sacred? In the Church's experience, the answer must be no, at least for our fallen humanity. Since the very beginning of Christianity, the temptation to turn a profit from the gifts freely given us by Christ have always been present. And ever since Judas sold Our Lord for thirty pieces of silver, there have been those who have succumbed to the temptation.

1 Simon Magus, as we are told in the Acts of the Apostles, was so impressed with what the apostles were able to do because of the gifts of the Holy Spirit that he wanted to purchase those same gifts for himself. The

assumption is that such a gift, once purchased, would be very profitable for the one who possessed it. We see the tendency to simony in our own time in preachers or leaders of religious movements who use their position as a way to attain material advancement or personal influence.

Named in honor of their founding sinner, simonists (or simoniacs) put forward the false front of piety and concern for the spiritual, but they merely use the spiritual as a means of attaining the material. The higher becomes a means of attaining something lower: they've turned the proper order of things upside down. Simony wasn't just a matter of profiting from the sacraments but also from the allocation of Church offices: the selling of benefices to the highest bidder rather than to someone to whom the spiritual goals of the Church could rightly be entrusted. What underlies all of these varieties of simony is the idea that spiritual realities can be bought and sold. What the panderers did to sexual love, the simoniacs did to the love of God.

13 From his vantage point at the center of the bridge over the third malebolgia, Dante again notices the "livid iron stone" that forms these trenches. Even though each of these sorts of sins is different from the others, there is something they all have in common: a certain cold-bloodedness or malice in pursuing their objects.

Dante is able to see that the trench's walls and floor are full of holes, holes that call to his mind the baptismal font in the baptistry in his native Florence. The sacramental imagery is intentional. These souls have used sacred things for profit, and those same sacred things become a means of their punishment.

25 The punishment of the simoniacs is complex in its symbolism.

Their being upside down allows us to see only their legs, from just above the knee. They had deceived people by presenting the higher, spiritual things to them, while they were looking for something lower. Here the lower is the only part of them that can be seen. Their deception has been exposed.

The fire burning on the soles of the feet calls to mind various aspects of the sin. The flames call to mind the flame of faith that each baptized Christian received at baptism. Probably even more important for the sin being punished here, the fire also reminds us of the tongues of fire burning over the heads of the apostles at Pentecost, fire which was an outward sign of the gift of the Holy Spirit which had been bestowed upon them. "As flame upon a thing anointed goes . . ." This suggests the anointing with oil on the hands the bishops and priests received at their own ordinations.

These images are inverted because the simonists inverted the proper order of things: "Whoever you may be whose up is down" (line 46). They trod underfoot the holy things, and so this burning oil now burns their feet. The very instrument of their receiving the Holy Spirit and the sacramental powers they lusted after and abused is now the instrument of their suffering.

One further aspect of the punishment still remains undisclosed: these souls are being squeezed into the rock itself by their successors. This suffering becomes known to Dante only later, as he speaks with a soul who mistakes him for Pope Boniface VIII. Dante is clearly of the opinion that an exalted position in the Church is no guarantee of holiness. Dante will introduce his readers to many bishops and popes in hell. What matters at the time of judgment is not our title but the charity in our souls.

34   In order to converse with these upside-down souls, Virgil and Dante are going to descend by the lower bank into the trench itself. Virgil actually carries Dante up and down these banks, which Dante would be unable to negotiate on his own.

52   This soul mistakes Dante for someone he is expecting—Pope Boniface VIII, a pope for whom Dante had very little sympathy. The soul is perplexed because the damned's knowledge of the future is usually accurate, and he isn't expecting Boniface for a few years yet! Perhaps that confusion is the reason he repeats himself. It also gives him an opportunity to reveal some of Boniface's supposed faults. History gives us no clear picture of Boniface selling Church goods or offices. Perhaps what Dante has in mind is that Pope Boniface used his ecclesiastical power for political ends in his struggles with Florence. Using his power to sanctify for ends that are not supernatural would qualify as the sort of inversion of priorities that Dante sees as the defining characteristic of simony.

61   Virgil encourages Dante to explain, in what might seem like an act of sympathy. The soul, Pope Nicholas III, is confused because his knowledge of the future

seems to have been inaccurate. One would expect, if this were true, that the soul would be relieved as soon as Dante had explained who he really was. Far from being relieved, this new information causes Nicholas distress: "The spirit writhed and wrenched his feet and, sighing, with a voice of grief and tears . . ." Was causing this distress really Virgil's intention from the beginning? The reason for this distress will become clear later.

72   In the same way that Nicholas had "stashed" the proceeds from his simony, here he himself is stashed in this hole. He lived as though lining his pockets was all that mattered. Here he symbolizes that misconception forever.

73   Aside from the fire burning on the soles of their feet, there is a second layer of punishment for the simonists, a sort of parody of the apostolic succession they abused in order to make a profit. These ecclesiastics received their sacramental powers and jurisdiction from the Church, by the laying on of hands. Their power is a direct result of their sacramental connection with the apostles. They are who they are because they are part of a succession. Real succession is necessary.

This same sort of succession is present in their punishment. Here they keep the light burning on the soles of their feet until their successor comes; this is perhaps why Nicholas was upset to learn that Dante wasn't Boniface—perhaps when he comes, Nicholas will hand on the task of keeping the flame alive to him and his soles will no longer be on fire. But, when his successor does come, although the fire will no longer punish him, he will follow his predecessors, "squashed flat into the fissure of the stone." The Church is intended to be built *upon* the Rock, but here these abusers of Church authority are built *into* the rock, going lower and lower until the end of time.

> SAINT Catherine of Siena lived in the time when the pope had left Rome and moved to the relative safety of southern France, in the beautiful city of Avignon. She was convinced that the Bishop of Rome needed to be in the Eternal City, regardless of the risks. She wrote to the pope; she organized a delegation to visit him in Avignon. She was relentless. And her determination had an effect: he returned to Rome. Her love for the Church did not force her into silence, but it did affect the way she spoke. Even when threatening and correcting, Catherine referred to the pope as sweet vicar of Christ, or as the sweet Christ on earth. The fact that he was, despite his weakness, the vicar of Christ demanded respect. But the very same fact required him to live according to a higher set of principles. Catherine was exceptionally clear in remembering both the respect due the office and the responsibilities that came with it as well.

82 Dante is being very controversial in condemning such recent popes as Boniface VIII and Clement V to hell.

But he sees them as betrayers of the sacred trust given to them, people who have degraded the supernatural calling of the Church by using their power to advance their political and earthly position. He puts the words of condemnation into the mouths of the souls in hell, but it still must have been a dangerous thing for him to write. This "prophecy" about Boniface VIII coming to hell at the end of his life is made possible by the fact that Dante is writing much later about a journey at the turn of the century, when Boniface was still alive.

90 Dante is clearly filled with indignation at Nicholas, and lashes out at him, asking how much money Christ required of St. Peter before he gave him the keys, or how much the apostles charged Matthias for entry into their company. "Then stay right where you are, you're punished well!" Dante says the only curb on his words is the fact that "I'm ruled by reverence for those highest keys."

We have learned to our sorrow in recent years that love for the Church cannot be used as an excuse for remaining silent about abuses within it. Love has driven many saints to denounce these wrongs precisely because they are cancers deforming and sapping strength from the Church they live for and would willingly die for. Dante seems to have some of that same zeal.

106 Dante interprets the prophecy of the Whore of Babylon as representing a Church who has abandoned her

true spouse (Christ himself) and has given herself to earthly kings. Mixing the sacred and the profane is the cause of much of the corruption in society, according to Dante. Both the ecclesiastical and the political have their proper domains. The world is a better place when that distinction is maintained. Some sort of distinction between Church and State is needed for the protection of both. Whether this is really the same thing as that "separation of Church and State" that the founders of the American Constitution had in mind is unclear. Dante, it seems clear, would not have been troubled in the nineteenth century when the Church lost control of the papal states. The modern Church, he would probably argue, has the moral authority it does precisely because it has lost any pretense of earthly power.

121 Virgil recognizes the importance of what Dante says. Protection of the distinction between the sacred and the temporal powers is necessary for the health of the Church (which matters to the believer) but also for the health of society (which any human being can recognize).

CANTO 20

Marketing Hope

In the United States in 2016, the *reported earnings* for spiritualists of various sorts exceeded two billion dollars. The industry has been expanding rapidly since the economic downturn. Perhaps it seems odd that a society that has little room for God and religion pays so much attention to (and money for) astrologers, palm readers, and spiritualists. But it should not. When life is uncertain and we feel afraid, we want nothing more than a reassurance that the future will be better or otherwise advice for how to change it. For past generations, our trust in God and his providence calmed our fears and anxieties. When that has been lost, with what are we left? With people willing to make a profit from our insecurities.

9 ". . . as slow and solemn as a litany." The ecclesiastical tone that Dante adopts here is intentional. These sinners treated the "signs" they interpreted with the sort of respect due to God alone. They were the "high

priests" of these false natural signs of the future. The tone of this canto will be echoed in canto 23, where we will see hypocrites moving in a similar slow procession. They, too, were false priests.

11. The twisting of the heads backwards ("miraculously screwed about") is what defines the punishment of these diviners—those who tried to see the future. How is this appropriate to their sin? A punishment can be appropriate to a sin in two different ways: by denying the soul the very thing they sought to acquire or by giving them exactly what they want (if that's what you *really* want, here you go!). The first way is what we usually associate with punishment and is often called retribution. In Dante's picture of hell, the punishments are more frequently of the second sort: the sin itself has become our punishment.

This punishment of the diviners might appear retributive because these souls wanted to see the future, but now all they can see is what is behind them: ". . . for they had lost the sight of things ahead" (15). What they suffer seems to be exactly the opposite of what they were seeking.

In another way, their punishment can be interpreted as the embodiment of their sin. These souls wanted to know the future, wanted security about what was to come. But that knowledge, that security, comes only by turning towards God, because the truth of the future exists only in God's mind—as part of his eternal plan. These people turned towards God's creatures rather than to the creator. They wanted knowledge and security but looked in the wrong direction. And they offered to others the security of "knowing the future" instead of the trust that every creature owes his loving maker, turning their attention (and their devotion) to the stars and other natural forces created by God instead of towards God himself, who is provident over everything. They have managed to get things "so wholly twisted round" (17).

22 ". . . our human image there / so gone awry and twisted . . ." This is clearly true in the physical sense—the pathway of the trickling tears of the sinners makes this twistedness graphically clear. But it is true in a spiritual sense as well. We are made in God's image. We are his, entirely dependent upon him, but we try to find our answers to our anxieties by turning *away* from him rather than *to* him. He is the way, but we've walked looking away from him, backwards.

28 "Here pity lives the best when it is dead." Virgil immediately corrects Dante for his weeping, suggesting that Dante is a fool like all the others. The sin of these souls is so fundamental (leading others to turn away from trusting God's providence) that they don't deserve Dante's pity. Pity is meant to move us to help those who need our help. But these souls have rejected the very source of hope by turning from God and leading others to do the same.

30 Anthony Esolen, in his note on this passage, suggests,

"We should note also that none of the soothsayers speak. Perhaps the wrenching of the throat forbids it" (p. 476). It is fitting that these false and misleading voices be silenced.

38   As we have already seen, in one sense, the punishment is an embodiment of their twisted crime, but, in another sense, it is retributive. They tried to look too far forward, and now they are forced to look backward instead. Which does Dante intend? He very well might intend both!

100 Dante seems almost to be humoring Virgil about his rather extensive account of the founding of his hometown of Mantua. Virgil's explanation makes all others appear like "extinguished coals." Dante almost seems to be saying, "I realize that you are from Mantua, *but* could we pay attention to the souls passing by, please? Are any of these of interest?" Despite the ingenuity of Virgil's explanation, "My mind keeps coming back to that alone."

117 Are diviners being punished because they looked for answers in the wrong places or because they were frauds? With Dante's description of Michael Scot, the famous astrologer and alchemist from the court of Frederick II, the fraudulence of divining is clearly acknowledged: he "play[ed] the tricks of sorcery."

121 The "sad women" sound like a more complicated case. Were their spells sincere? If their attempts at telling the

future were believed by themselves, then how are they frauds? If they were sincere, who were they deceiving?

If it is just for these women to be punished here (and that must be the assumption, since God's justice is always done), then their fortune-telling *must* have been fraudulent in some way. Fraud requires a culpable deception. Somehow they must *know* that what they are saying is false. Perhaps they are simply con artists. That is certainly possible, and the case of Michael Scot is presented as an example of simple deception. But perhaps with these women, we're facing a sort of *self*-deception, in which they culpably embrace a falsehood because it satisfies some desire in them, a desire to be thought special and spiritual, or perhaps a desire to have security by knowing what the future will bring. Perhaps this self-deceiving divining is like an "easy button" we are tempted to push rather than do the hard and constant work of trusting God.

CANTO 21

Society Serving the Selfish
Fighting Back Without Diminishing Ourselves
A Culture of "Fine Print"

John Dalberg-Acton, the first Baron Acton, had the opportunity to observe power up close. His experience has been passed on to future generations in the memorable quotation, "Power tends to corrupt; absolute power corrupts absolutely." A person's moral conscience tends to diminish as his power increases. It is a rare and beautiful thing to meet someone in power who is humbled and honored to serve his city or country. Public service is usually interpreted in our fallen world as the public serving the official, not the other way around.

1   The relationship between Dante and Virgil is not reducible to their journey through hell. Part of their conversation is private, not for our ears.

16   Like the shipbuilding yards in Venice, this malebolgia or ditch is filled with tarry pitch, boiling by no earthly power, leaving the banks of the pit covered in a sticky coating (18). The picture is one of great darkness, but also of a sort of contaminating stickiness, a filth that attaches itself to everything. The surface of the tar reveals nothing besides the thick bubbles that rise, grow, and burst (21). Stickiness and concealment of what hides beneath the surface seem to be the predominant images.

22   Dante's staring into the tarry pit is interrupted by Virgil's cry: "Look out!" Up to now, except for the gates of Dis, Virgil has encouraged Dante to be courageous, not to let fear keep him from facing up to the horrors of hell. But here, Virgil himself sounds panicky. He's spotted a devil dashing at them by the double propulsion of both feet and wide-spread wings. The devil is as black as the tarry pit he patrols. And he is one of many devils, called by Dante *Malebranche*, literally Evilclaws. These devils have been given outlandish names, and their interactions are fascinating (and at times hilarious). But make no mistake, they are vicious. The fear they inspire is an essential part of the tone of this canto: this is a chaotic place where terror reigns.

Until now in their journeys, Dante and Virgil have witnessed punishments that are somehow the natural outcome of the sins committed. The imagery has carefully avoided the typical picture of hell: devils poking sinners with pitchforks. And now we find the pitchforks! But why now? Why does the punishment here include these armed devils?

34   It turns out that Dante and Virgil are not the devil's target. He is transporting a soul, carrying him by the Achilles tendons, like game that's been strung up. This is a distinctively predatory place, and the souls are the prey. The souls are treated merely as sport for the devils, objects for their entertainment.

42   These souls are barrators or grafters—those who have abused their position in public office for their own personal advancement, usually financial. They have presented themselves to the world as public servants but are in fact using the public for their own private gain; they have come not to serve but to be served. Concern for their own personal profit, rather than for the common good they are called to protect, can turn "no" into "of course." All it takes is the right enticement or bribe. For much of Italian history, this sin has been developed into an art form.

Now that we have discovered who is being punished in the pit, we can see part of the reason the devils are involved in the punishment. These souls have abused the civic power with which they were entrusted. They objectified their subjects, using their power (both influence and force, usually in the form of "enforcers") to extract whatever it was they wanted. And now these souls are pawns in the game. Understood in this way, the punishment is clearly retributive.

We shall see that there is more to their punishment than mere retribution, however. What they experience here in the tar is in some real way reflective of how they lived while on earth.

43   The soul dashes away from the demon, diving into the tar. When even part of him is visible, he is threatened with attack by hooks. Given the slightest opportunity, the devils attack: they "harpooned him with a hundred prongs" (52). The imagery suggests that here you are never safe; there is no relaxing or letting down the guard. These souls are like mice with a cat waiting outside their hole.

53   The connection between the punishment and the sin is made clearer here: these souls were masters of working "undercover," under the table, under the radar: "You do your jigs here undercover." Success in their sinful ways on earth required them to avoid detection from higher authorities by remaining out of sight. Being exposed to view must be avoided at all costs. Here they must do the same: work out of sight, with only the bubbles in the tar to tell us that anyone is there at all. Revealing even the smallest part of their bodies can be the cause of horrible punishment.

These were souls who abused authority, but they were also subject to authority. They might have acted as though they were a law unto themselves, but they were not. They were mere "middle management," taking what they could while remaining undetected by the big boss. Somehow it can all seem like a game.

58　This place is lawless enough that Virgil, usually a voice pushing Dante to courage, instructs him to hide behind a rock. When society disintegrates so far as this, rational discourse is of no use, and fear and constant vigilance are the only rational responses. Remember Virgil at the gates of the city of Dis, when his command to let them in went unheeded. The same bewilderment will happen again soon when he realizes that the Evilclaws have lied to him about there being a bridge over the malebolgia of the hypocrites.

　　Virgil needs to be as crafty as the devils to make it through. He's no longer an all-knowing tour guide, the one with all the answers, always in control of the situation; here he is just an inexperienced player in a sort of reality game in which he needs to keep his wits about him. So often, in a corrupt society, even honest people need, or feel the need, to "play the game" in order to survive.

67　Intimidation is the norm here. The devils instill fear just as the public officials who find themselves in hell used their position to intimidate those subject to them. Fear is used as a tool of manipulation, to lessen the resistance of others, to wear them down. These devils are stereotypical bullies.

78　Even the devils are aware that they have to be on guard and be at the top of their game. They, too, can be fooled and manipulated. In this game of cat and mouse, the roles are not clearly defined. As we'll see, here the predator can swiftly become the prey. Esolen sums up the tone of the struggle beautifully when he writes, "Theirs is the game of the naked and shifty against the armed and stupid, world without end" (p. 480). In a strange way, the devils are being punished here along with the souls they torment. They aren't really in charge. They are often frustrated in their desires and ineffective in their attempts to control the souls punished here.

79   Virgil immediately puts the devil called Eviltail in his place. He and Dante are here and have passed through many obstacles on the way here because it has been willed by God. Even the Evilclaws operate under authority. Their bullying is not entirely unrestrained. They aren't the "top dog."

87   "There won't be any stabbing now." The devil's disappointment is evident as he drops his grappling hook. The game, at least for the moment, is over for him; he's a stupid thug who's been caught. The devils' authority is clearly not absolute. They aren't rulers of this malebolgia, but residents, too. The petty official, in this case Eviltail, has been caught red-handed by the big boss. In the face of *real* authority, the abuse of his own authority has to stop. His "toy" has been taken away, and he pouts like a child.

BULLYING and intimidation have a dehumanizing effect. Even if we try to pay no attention, the constant threat

> wears us down. Even if we try not to react, we find frustration and anger growing inside of us. Before we know it, we are giving as good as we get; we have allowed ourselves to be dragged down to their thuggish level. We are playing their game. How do we stand up to these bullies without losing our own moral sense and dignity?

97   The dehumanizing effects of intimidation and fear are clear in the picture Dante paints of himself: "I pressed myself close to my leader's side from head to toe, and never let my eyes turn from their faces." Intimidation intends to produce a loss of dignity in its subjects. They are made to feel that resistance is useless. In Dante's case, the fear is well-founded, since the Evilclaws are continually bantering among themselves about what they are going to do to him. He has already seen what they did to the souls punished here. Can he trust their words and promises? In a place like this, there is no trust, and, as a result, no rest. The weak must always be on guard against the powerful.

106   The Evilclaws weave together truth and deception in a dangerous way. They explain that the bridge here is out because of an event they are able to time down to the hour: the earthquake at Our Lord's death. This fits with what Virgil and Dante already know about damage done to the landscape of hell through the paschal mystery. Remember, however, that Virgil's other journey here was before that time; he hasn't seen this damage to the bridge firsthand. The likelihood of what the

devils tell him, however, inclines him to believe them. So, when the devil tells him that there is a bridge not much further along the ditch that is still intact (110), Virgil believes that too.

115 The devils even appear to offer to be helpful, serving as guides for the travelers, guaranteeing them safe passage. Is this cooperative spirit the result of Virgil's words about their being here on God's authority? Perhaps they had more effect than he thought at first? Are the Evilclaws bending their wills to the inevitable and voluntarily obeying God's will? In this circle, with these particular sinners, cooperation is never what it appears to be. Words are used as a means to an end, a selfish end. Circumstances are made to be taken advantage of, and these devils are just the sort to grab hold of that advantage.

118 The extravagant names of the Evilclaws make them even more ridiculous. It is hard to take someone named Stormbreath seriously, even if he has tusks. These are not "superior" beings but thugs, violent and intimidating, but ultimately stupid and laughable. Here we see what happens when we allow "might" to be equivalent to "right."

"READ the fine print" is usually a reminder that hidden under the surface of the agreement is something unpleasant that you do not expect: some hidden charges, or the cancellation of a benefit for arbitrary reasons. Contracts

> and agreements are intended to be clear and binding, not a means of manipulation and deception. When Our Lord's disciples questioned him about making oaths, he demanded clear, unequivocal speech from them: "Let what you say be simply 'Yes' or 'No'; anything more than this comes from the Evil One" (Mt 5:37).

125 "Keep these men safe until that other ridge, the one that crosses all the dens intact." The devil is as good as his word. Virgil and Dante will be safe with this hellish patrol, all the way to the bridge that is still standing. But what effect does this guarantee have if there *is* no bridge? I suppose no one suspects that the devils are logicians.

127 Dante, picking up the signals from the Evilclaws (it's hard to ignore the fact that they are drooling and grinning, making faces at one another), pleads with Virgil that the two of them would be safer making their way by themselves. But Virgil, desiring to believe them, desiring to believe in God's authority even here, overrules him. Virgil thinks that all of this posturing by the devils is really intended for the souls of the fraudulent officials, not the two of them. Here we see the destructive power of fraud. Rational people *want* to believe in the basic goodness of their neighbors; our society depends upon the ability to take one another at our word. Virgil, the voice of reason, refuses to give up on that confidence in the truthfulness of other rational beings. It is Virgil's basic goodness that they are manipulating.

CANTO 22

The Ultimate Weakness of Evil
The Disintegrating Power of Evil

When early philosophers tried to explain the possibility of evil in the world, they concluded that there must be two causes of the universe we see, one who is good and another who is evil. These two causes must be equal in power; otherwise one would have won the battle between them by now. This theory is called "dualism" because it holds the existence of two independent, eternal causes. The evil cause must be an impressive reality if it is capable of dueling an all-powerful and good God to a draw.

But evil is not like this. Lucifer and the other fallen angels, the devil and his minions, left their glory behind when they rebelled against God. What remains in them is still powerful, but it is also both despicable and laughable. And even if they were not corrupted by their fall, they are merely creatures of God; he made them, holds them in being, and uses them for his purposes. Do not romanticize them as much literature has done.

1   The previous canto ends and this one begins with what is obviously a display of "bathroom humor." The devils are called into action by an unexpected sort of trumpet call: "And he had made a bugle of his arse." This provides some of the only comic relief we will be granted on our journey through hell.

Perhaps this is a subtle reminder that those who abuse their positions of authority, although they might insist upon displays of respect and shows of status, are in fact ridiculous figures. These thuggish devils are the sort of underlings that the corrupt officials might have hired while they were in power during their lives on earth, but these "civic leaders" would never have associated with them in other ways. Here the "lowlifes" have taken control, and the sophisticated grafters have no choice but to humor them, obey when necessary, and to maneuver to stay clear of them. These devils, ignorant and brutish though they may be, treat the sinners here with a sort of contempt. They provide for the sinners a most personal revelation of what each of them did to those under their authority on earth. Regardless of how highly these men of rank thought of themselves while alive, underneath it all, they were like these devils.

22   These corrupt officials worked under cover; their actions were hidden from the public view, covert. Here

they continue in the mode of living they cultivated on earth. They must stay below the surface, out of sight. Disclosure is to be avoided whenever possible. What matters is not being seen, not getting caught. It is only for the briefest of moments, in order to lessen their pain, that they reveal themselves at all. They will break the surface, like frogs in the shallows of a pond, but, like the frogs, dive when one of the devils approaches.

31 He who is too much in the open quickly becomes prey for the devils. One unfortunate soul is captured by Dogscratcher, one of the Malebranche, who quickly makes him the center of a cruel game, like cats playing with an injured mouse. "'Claw him and strip the leather from his back!' the cursed demons hollered all together." They play with him like those in power often seem to toy with those powerless subjects who fall into their clutches. The public is seen, not as the master, some *one* whose good must be served, but as an object, some *thing* for the entertainment and enrichment of the official. The sin of civic corruption objectifies the public that is supposed to be served. Here we see most clearly the fraudulence of corruption. These officials were given positions of authority in order to protect the common good but use that very authority for their private good.

53 We see the method of these grafters in the poor soul from Navarre. He is here for accepting bribes. He'd bleed people for as much as he could get. Here he gets a

feel for the sort of treatment he dishes out, for the powerlessness of being manipulated, of being made sport of. He is at the mercy of the devils and gets gored by Swinetooth and is saved by Curlybeard, only because he wants to save the fun for himself: "Keep clear, you! Mine's the fork for this one here" (60). There is no mercy, just predators fighting over their supper. The soul from Navarre is not treated as a someone, but as the property of Swinetooth and Curlybeard.

62   Curlybeard seems willing to let the captured soul talk. As the cat lets the trapped mouse run around a bit, he's confident he'll get him sooner or later. Perhaps it's part of the punishment of this sort of sinner to be exposed, to have to talk. Having to "name names" is a sort of punishment in itself for those who are accustomed to working underground.

SUPERHEROES are often sent into battle against evil masterminds. We picture this evil force as well-prepared and moving like a finely tuned machine. But evil does not work that way. It is fundamentally disordered.

Virtues are habits that help direct our powers towards their proper targets, acting in accordance with reason. Since all of the virtues have the same goal, they focus our powers together, integrating our personality, making it whole. But evil desires chase after their own obsessions, pulling us in whatever direction. We are in the center of a moral tug-of-war. Keeping control over all of these disorderly powers often feels like herding cats: both

> exhausting and ultimately futile. No wonder Saint Paul described what it feels like to have a fallen human nature in these words: "I do not understand my own actions. For I do not do what I want, but I do the very thing I hate" (Rom 7:15). Sin dis-integrates our personality.

70   There certainly isn't any honor among thieves in hell. There seems to be respect neither for one another nor for any sort of "rules of engagement." Stormbreath gets tired of all the talking and rips the soul with his grappling hook. The others are just about to join in as well. Any semblance of order dissolves almost immediately. Chaos is always lurking in the background. When there is no rule of law, no one is safe. Anyone stronger can attack and take away what you have; that is true even for the demons. It is only by force that the Evilclaws can defend what they perceive to be theirs. Notice that, in a "society" like this, no one, not even the bad guys, can rest safe.

77   "My leader did not pause." In a disorderly society, you can never know that you'll get a chance again, so you are forced to grab your opportunities when they come. The unpredictability of life means that you need to be aggressive and assertive, snatching what you can get while you can get it, attributes that might be necessary in the wild, but hardly contribute to civilized life.

82   Here the connection between graft and the breakdown of the bond of society is vividly portrayed.

Taking bribes led this sinner to betray his master by releasing his master's enemies. Everyone, seeing the action from the outside, thought that he was motivated by mercy and a striving for holiness, forgiving even his enemies, but in reality, the bribe was all that moved him. The lower, selfish motive was masquerading as something noble.

91 The discussion gets cut off because a new threat has come into view: "That other demon bares his fangs!" Again we see the disruptive effects of the disorder here. We can't even carry on a conversation without having to drop everything to respond to a new threat.

96 Look at the lack of respect between the Malebranche: "Get over there, you filthy crow!" They do not look upon each other as glorious creatures or important operatives in a carefully planned mission. Those who had been glorious angels are now thought of, even by their own, as dirty birds.

97 Even though this soul from Navarre who had been seized by the devils has suffered terribly already, he's still in the game, still trying to talk his way out of trouble. By offering to give the "all clear" signal to his fellow corrupt officials and call them to the surface (either so that they can speak to Dante or so that the devils can snatch them, depending upon which lines you focus on), he gets the Evilclaws to withdraw. He'll say whatever it takes to get what he wants. They fall for it, like macho men who can't bear not to accept a challenge

or dare. The deceptive corrupt official knows that and uses it to his advantage. We are reminded that the devils aren't really in charge; there is a constant struggle between the crafty crooks themselves and the brutal devils who patrol them. The devils seem to be just as much one of the punished as one of the punishers.

107 "It's all a trick." Yes, it *is* all a trick; the question is, however, a trick upon whom? Is the fast-talking official tricking the demon or his fellow sufferers? When he admits to being an "evil trickster," he doesn't make matters any clearer, does he? He wants the Evilclaws to think that he is betraying his fellow souls, which he certainly might have done in the past. Here there is no such thing as a stable alliance. No one is on *your* side, because it is definitely "each man for himself."

112 Harlequin, another one of the Evilclaws, lets his own pride lead him astray. He falls for the trick because he thinks he'll be able to win. It isn't merely a matter of people *knowing* what you are doing is wrong; what really counts is whether they can catch you. Not getting caught becomes a sort of game, what Dante calls "this new sport."

124 The man makes good his escape, at which the devils, poor fools that they are, seem surprised. But rather than cutting their losses, they pursue him, in a race between fear and shame. Fear wins, but only with an "assist" from one of the devils, who wants to start a fight. The devil actually turns on the pursuer, attacking

and being attacked by talons, until both fall into the pitch. The canto ends with two sticky, humiliated devils being hauled out of the tar by the very hooks they used to torture the corrupt officials. In this sort of disorder, no one wins.

CANTO 23

Evil Is Never Unpunished
The Christian Life Frees Us From Burdens
Joyless "Saints"
Walking With a Clear Conscience

Life can seem very unfair. People who break the rules and take advantage of others appear to be the ones who get noticed and get ahead. This world seems to reward cheaters and complainers, the squeaky wheels who always get the grease. Although there are some instances of these cheaters receiving their just punishment, often we are left to contemplate what seems like a very unjust world. Christians can trust that God's justice is always achieved. Whether through the sufferings of the next life or from the twistedness that sin causes even now, crime never goes unpunished.

1. Dante and Virgil begin their solitary search for the intact bridge in a solemn, almost ecclesiastical, manner. They walk like friars in single file. This quasi-liturgical

tone helps to prepare us for the following ditch where we will find one liturgical theme after another, because so many of the sinners there not only *were* clerics but used their status in a fraudulent way and so find themselves in the pit of the hypocrites.

4   Dante compares the scene at the end of the previous canto, with devils covered in tar, to one of Aesop's fables, the one about the frog and the mouse. The frog agrees to help the mouse across a stream but secretly plans to kill him. But a bird, seeing the mouse struggling in the water, swoops down to snatch the mouse and gets the frog as well. The trouble the frog got the mouse into ended up being trouble for the frog as well. The moral of the fable is that evil intentions are punished. In the same way, the devil Tramplefrost's attack against his fellow devil Harlequin didn't result in a victory for the attacker but defeat for both of them. They both ended up "cooked beneath the crust" and in a "tangled mess."

13 Dante's instincts tell him that the Evilclaws will seek vengeance for their humiliation at being tricked by the escaping sinner and ending up stuck in the boiling tar themselves. Dante is accustomed to dealing with officials suffering from wounded pride! As they walk along the edge between the two ditches, he gets more and more apprehensive, a feeling shared by Virgil. Notice that Dante is the one who takes the initiative here. He is more accustomed to the rough-and-tumble life

of corrupt politics. Virgil clearly defers to him as the expert on the subject, mirroring Dante's thoughts like a "pane of leaded glass" (25). They discuss their strategy, a slightly undignified slide into the next ditch, but are interrupted.

34 Seeing the Evilclaws approaching with obviously evil intent, Virgil grabs Dante and, holding him against his chest, slides down the rocky slope into the trench of the hypocrites. At least in part, their exit has a purely dramatic function, a way of escaping from imminent danger, but it also suggests that one cannot (and perhaps should not) reason with those who abuse power—avoidance is the best strategy. Do whatever it takes to put distance between yourself and them.

40 The paternal care Virgil displays for Dante gets repeated mention. Virgil is like a mother fleeing a fire with her child, without thought for herself, only thinking about saving her child. This relationship is put into less figurative words later: ". . . not as his fellow or friend, but as his son" (51).

55 The devils' power is strictly limited—they cannot go beyond the banks of their particular ditch. They are like county police who reach the county line and cannot pursue beyond it. The demons are just as much imprisoned here as are the souls they torment. What they do, even the pain they inflict, is part of God's providence; they could do nothing if he did not allow it. They wanted to rule, to be like God, but they are

sentenced to eternity being "middle-management" in a tarry pit, acting as instruments of Divine justice, a sort of indentured servitude in hell.

58. "We found a painted populace." Before we find out what the sin is which is being punished here, Dante lets the imagery begin to "paint the picture." This is yet another example of Dante's "front-loading" of images.

Dante has already set a liturgical tone with his talk of their single-file walk being like a procession of friars. Here we come to learn that this is a painted populace, one whose exterior is artificial, not necessarily reflecting the reality beneath. This disjunction between the visible exterior and hidden interior is a recurring theme in this canto.

> OUR LORD told his disciples, "For my yoke is easy, and my burden is light" (Mt 11:30). There are few passages from the Gospel that Christians show forth less in their lives than this one. We tend to view the spiritual life as something heroic and difficult; it is ultimately worth doing because of the eternal promises given to us, but in the meantime it is a sacrifice, hard work. But there is something fundamentally wrong about this attitude, something unchristian. If we find the Christian life basically burdensome, we are living it incorrectly. We have been set free from so many different burdens. Perhaps it takes a trip through hell to recognize just how heavy a life of sin truly is. "Lord, by your cross and resurrection, you have set us free" (Memorial Acclamation at Mass).

59   The next layer of imagery concerns the burdensomeness of their existence. Their steps are slow; they weep as they go; their expressions communicate exhaustion. Whatever it is they are doing (and the observer isn't immediately sure), it is drudgery. Later (in line 67) we'll hear: "O weary mantle for eternity." We don't yet

know the reason for the burdensomeness of their existence, merely the fact of it.

61 Next, Dante adds another ecclesiastical note—they are dressed in copes like the monks of Cluny, with hoods that obscure their faces. The monastic hoods were intended to promote a freedom from distraction, a sort of holy "tunnel vision." Here the purpose is different: obscuring the wearer from view. This obscurity, as we'll see, is both descriptive of their sin but also part of their ordeal.

64 Finally, we discover that these copes are golden on the outside (whether plated or painted, we aren't certain) but lead beneath. The image this calls to mind, especially to someone of Dante's time, is of a counterfeit coin.

Lead was used by counterfeiters and by alchemists to simulate gold because it is malleable like gold (think of people biting coins to see if they are soft enough to bear the marks of their teeth, as gold would), but primarily because it is of comparable weight (or density, to be precise). Even in the modern periodic table, gold and lead are close neighbors, very similar in atomic weight. Lead has the weight or heaviness of gold, but little or none of the value: this is what is central to the imagery here.

70 Again, the burden and the tiredness are the focus, but now we know the reason: their glittering garments are unthinkably heavy. This is a perfect image of how these hypocrites deformed religion. The practice of

their religion was intended by God to lift a burden from their shoulders. "My yoke is easy and my burden is light." These sinners have deformed the divine intention of religion, interpreting it merely as a series of obligations that placed ever more burdens upon men. Somehow, these hypocrites (we should think of the scribes and Pharisees whom Our Lord labeled with precisely this sin) have managed to get the purpose of religion entirely backwards.

72 This weight upon their shoulders makes these souls terribly slow-moving. This allows Dante and Virgil to move past many of them, looking for anyone they might recognize. This personal recognition of familiar faces doesn't happen—perhaps this is a result of the obscurity mentioned in line 61. Hypocrites did their religious actions in order to be noticed, so that men could see, but here their identities are hidden by their golden hoods. Someone, however, recognizes Dante's Tuscan accent. He is the one recognized, not the souls being punished. The souls are required to remain hidden, something they refused to do in the religious life on earth, where they were called upon to "pray in secret, and the Father, who sees in secret, will reward you."

82 Two souls hasten to meet Dante, a haste of the will rather than of the feet—they just can't go any faster than they are presently moving.

89 ". . . by what privilege . . ." Even here the souls are

very aware of the human respect given to others. They seem bothered that someone has received a privilege not given to them. Questions of preeminence are still at the front of their minds. They want to sit at the best seats at table, in the front pew of the synagogue, and be recognized by men.

90 "The stole of lead" implies that this sin is particularly priestly, since the stole is the vestment which specifically identifies the priest. In a way, this malebolgia is a fitting neighbor to the grafters. The grafters abused their civil authority; their care for the common good was merely a cover for their own selfish ends. The hypocrites have abused their positions of honor in the Church; they used their spiritual status to attain earthly preferment. The very stoles that brought them respect when they wore them in the world are now the cause of their suffering.

> BELIEVING should bring us joy. But this proper fruit of belief is destroyed when religion is seen primarily as a list of obligations to be fulfilled rather than a loving service of a loving God. "Rejoice in the Lord always; again I will say, Rejoice!" (Phil 4:4). Joy is the side effect or natural by-product of Christian charity. There can be little charity where there is no joy.
>
> To maintain a proper attitude to religion, Saint Philip would command his followers to be cheerful. The world, he would say, had enough long-faced saints. In fact, the very expression is an oxymoron.

92 "... long-faced hypocrites ..." These hypocritical souls made a show on earth of the great work they did in the name of religion and want everyone to notice their fasting. But their long face was a lie and their religion hollow. It does not have true charity at its core. Here their deception is exposed.

110 Another layer of imagery is added to this liturgical procession of hypocrites clothed in lead. Dante is stopped mid-sentence when he catches sight of a man crucified on the ground, nailed directly into the ground (instead of being lifted up on high, as Our Lord was) by three nails. His suffering produces nothing uplifting, unlike Christ's. Christ's suffering was a triumph: "When I am lifted up, I will draw all men to myself." Not so with this man. Instead of offering words of inspiration in the midst of his suffering, as Our Lord did from the cross, he merely mutters into his beard.

The man is Caiaphas, the high priest at the time of Our Lord's crucifixion. He is the one (perhaps with the prophetic vision of his office) who saw that it was good for one man to suffer for the good of the people. Here he lies deep in hell, naked, crucified, and stretched across the path. He is walked upon by the lead-vested hypocrites, a sort of speed bump in the path of these already burdened souls. One can't help but think that he suffers horribly by being walked upon, but he is also the cause of suffering for others. He makes their passage more difficult as well by making them lift their feet higher to step on or over him. He is punished here because he imposed unnecessary burdens on people in life, and he continues to be a burden and an obstacle to others here in hell for eternity.

115 The significance of this is immediately explained to Dante by one of the hypocrites: "That soul . . . advised the Pharisees that it was fit to martyr one man for the people's sake." What Caiaphas had said is true: Christ

is destined to bear the weight of the sins of the entire world, which he did in the Garden of Gethsemane. The sacrifice of Jesus for the sake of sinners is part of God's plan for the salvation of the world.

Caiaphas, by virtue of his priestly office, spoke prophetically despite his bad intentions (again the interior reality and the exterior are at odds with each other). He was given the grace to see the truth but twisted that prophetic truth for his own end—staying in power. Now he is living out his own prophecy: *he* is bearing the weight of the sins of the scribes and Pharisees he was advising. While alive, he manipulated events behind the scenes, but here he lies exposed in all his nakedness. Shame and exposure are an essential part of his punishment.

121 Caiaphas is not alone bearing the heavy weight of the hypocrites. He shares his fate with Annas and the others who were in on the conspiracy to execute Jesus. They were sharers in his abuse of priestly power and the deceptive manipulation of the gift of prophecy.

> MOMENTS in our lives happen that are breakthroughs, almost revelations. Something we did not see clearly or understand fully is suddenly obvious to us. It is as though, like a modern-day Saint Paul, we feel the scales fall away from our eyes. Sometimes these moments of clarity come rather brutally, as when we make a fool of ourselves or are corrected publicly and humiliatingly. At other times, the awareness is given to us more gently, by God shining

> a quiet light in our souls during our prayer or in the sacrament of confession. But regardless of how they occur, these moments of recognition are often painful. First, we must face the embarrassment of our previous blindness; how is it even possible that I did not notice how wrong I was for all these years when it must have been perfectly obvious to everyone around me! Second, our new understanding calls us to conversion. Now that we see more clearly, we must live differently. Our newly enlightened conscience demands it. We must live in the truth.

124 Virgil is astonished and speechless, staring at the crucified Caiaphas. Part of his astonishment comes from the fact that the last time he passed through this malebolgia, the crucified high priests were not here. Virgil is accustomed to knowing his way around hell; he's the man with all the answers, the guide for Dante. Here he is surprised by the change that has occurred since his previous visit.

But there seems to be something more, something personal, something that strikes Virgil's conscience. Caiaphas is suffering so terribly here because he was entrusted with a prophetic gift, a gift that he used for evil purposes instead of the divine purpose for which it was intended. He was given the gift to see that Christ was to be the sacrifice for a sinful world, to see that he was the Messiah, and yet Caiaphas betrayed that special awareness entrusted to him.

Virgil, too, according to the medieval tradition,

had been given a prophetic gift. His writings had been seen as a special prophecy of the virgin birth, a sort of "proto-gospel," a message he could have received only as a divinely bestowed gift. And yet, despite this special information, despite his special treatment by God, he still had failed to give God the worship he deserved, failed to live up to the knowledge given to him. Perhaps Virgil saw in Caiaphas's punishment the punishment that he himself could have deserved. Perhaps Virgil is not such a "virtuous" pagan after all.

128 Immediately, Virgil asks about getting out of there! He is obviously disturbed by being there. This seems to confirm the fact that Virgil finds this malebolgia personally uncomfortable. He is disturbed because what he sees reveals something very important about himself. It is almost too painful to consider. His first instinct is to flee.

136 The bridges over this ditch are all broken: the Evilclaws were lying to Virgil. But why did the earthquake accompanying Our Lord's death destroy the bridges over the ditches here only and not elsewhere in the circle of fraud? They aren't materially or structurally different. The answer seems to lie with the sin punished here, and in particular with the priestly character of this canto.

In the ancient world, priests were often called by the title of *pontifex*. The pope still bears this title in a most exalted form: *pontifex maximus* (the highest pontifex). Pontifex etymologically means a builder of bridges. A priest is called by God to be a "pontifex" or bridge-builder between God and his people, a link between heaven and earth.

Caiaphas, Annas, and their coconspirators failed to be a bridge between their people and God, even when he was walking in their midst. They fell down on the job. Instead of acting as a bridge bringing the people to full belief in God's revelation, they set up roadblocks to following God incarnate. And so, in this pit, they are just that: obstacles in the road. The fallen bridges are symbols not only of their own failed priesthood but also of the old priesthood of Aaron being replaced by the one High Priest, Christ himself, who will be "the way" for all people. Christ's death, symbolized by the earthquake, establishes the new covenant, and with the new covenant and its new sacrifice, offered once and for all, a new priesthood is established. The old bridges have been demolished.

139 Virgil is visibly disturbed that the Evilclaws deceived him. Noble and upright people expect to be treated in an honest way. Is his anger merely because he expects a certain sort of treatment from others or because he is mortified to have been tricked by the likes of them? A wicked and hypocritical friar from Bologna hears the story of the deception and makes a comment that makes Virgil seem almost naive in trusting the demons in the first place: "I heard tell / of all the devil's vices, and I heard / that he was a liar and the father of lies." Why should Virgil expect otherwise?

CANTO 24

**Depending Upon the Opinions of Others
Stumbling Blocks and Stepping Stones
Perseverance on the Long Road
Financial Freedom and Freedom of Conscience**

We often burden ourselves psychologically and spiritually by judging ourselves according to the reactions of others. We examine ourselves in the mirror of their response to us and become addicted to their approval. But we all too often misinterpret the motives of others. *What did that comment mean?* We imagine that we are the focus of their thoughts and the target of their actions. But so often we are not their focus. This thinking "it is all about me" recalls a favorite scene from Casablanca. The con artist played by Peter Lorre is selling travel documents. His exchange with Rick (played by Humphrey Bogart) is painfully human in its self-centeredness. "'You despise me, don't you?' 'If I gave you any thought, I probably would.'"

1   Dante begins this canto with an extended image: frost that disappears at the rising of the sun. This might seem to be merely a sort of literary flourish on Dante's part. It certainly *is* that. He goes to great length to paint the picture for us, so much so that it is easy to forget the purpose of the image—Dante's mood has been strongly affected by Virgil's anger, leaving him "downcast for a while" (16). But that dark mood disappears like the frost in the sun when Virgil looks kindly at Dante.

It is easy to ignore the dramatic effects our own moods can have on those around us. We naturally reflect and respond to the emotional states of those we care about. We think that what we feel remains hidden inside of us, but we carry it on our faces as clearly as the anger was written on Virgil's brow.

> As we try to progress in the spiritual life, we expect, with our good intentions and firm resolutions, that life will cooperate with us. Somehow God will acknowledge the beginning we have made and offer a sign of his approval, a small reward for good behavior. And sometimes there are wonderful signs that confirm we are on the right path and God is with us. But often the path not only looks steep and difficult; it seems to disappear entirely. Where is God? What is he doing to me? The saints have experienced what they call spiritual desolation, a feeling of being abandoned by God. But even when he seems most distant (perhaps especially when he seems distant), he is

> working in a surprising way. What looks like a stumbling block becomes a stepping-stone. Everything, both what we find pleasant and what we find perplexing or hurtful, is a tool in the hands of God, shaping us into the saints we were created to be. "We know that in everything God works for good with those who love him" (Rom 8:28).

24 There is no way out of the ditch of the hypocrites except by climbing up the ruins of the collapsed bridge. This way out seems almost impossibly steep to Dante. Virgil's care for Dante, as he faces his fear of the climb out of the ditch and during the ascent itself, is more than a personal affection or charity: it is a symbol of the sort of care God lavishes upon us during our spiritual journey. As spiritual pilgrims, we don't always need to know the way, but to be confident that we, too, are being directed and assisted by a loving guide who is with us each step of the way.

Dante signifies this divine care first by "that sweet and gracious look" (20), showing the willingness and even eagerness with which God greets our pleas for help. We do not need to convince God to assist us; the initiative is his. He is more eager for our progress than we seem to be.

Dante then draws attention to how personal this care is by referring to Virgil's opening wide his arms and taking Dante by the hand (24). The help isn't to be some distant or abstract thing, a few commandments or chastisements now and then. God comes himself to help us, walking hand-in-hand. There is no greater manifestation of this truth than the Incarnation itself. God could perhaps have saved us in another way (Saint Thomas Aquinas certainly thought that he could), but God chose to become man because he desired to come *in person* to help us. His love for us could be expressed so vividly in no other way.

Finally, in line 29, we see Virgil giving Dante step-by-step directions, keeping him from giving in to his fears by making him focus on the immediate task at hand: "Cling tight to that one and climb up, / but test it first to see if it will hold" (29–30). In his providence, God arranges precisely what we need—no more, no less. We do not need to think about how long the path to holiness is. Our job is merely to take the *next* step, a step specially arranged by a loving God, and then to trust God on the remainder of the journey.

42 Providentially, the stones of the fallen bridge have become the stairs by which Virgil and Dante climb out of the pit of the hypocrites. Even when they oppose God, the hypocrites (and everyone else) still end up being instruments of God's plan of salvation. Even their rejection of the prophetic truth given to Caiaphas is used by God for good: it makes Virgil and Dante's trip possible. We'll see this holding true in the very pit of hell with Satan himself. No one escapes God's providence.

43 For anyone who has exerted himself to the very limits

of his abilities, the imagery of "my breath had been milked dry out of my lungs" will ring perfectly true.

> WE have come to expect immediate results, and we prefer those results with as little effort as possible! Our kitchens might be filled with "labor-saving devices," but there is no such thing in the spiritual life. Saint Paul refers to walking on the spiritual path as a fight or as running a race. Other authors call it a spiritual combat. One thing is clear: it is hard work, and if we want to go to heaven, we need to be prepared to exert ourselves. These battles or races might not be quick; they are often more like marathons than sprints. Be ready to persevere. "And let us run with perseverance the race marked out for us" (Heb 12:1).

46 "Shake off your sluggishness." One of the greatest obstacles in the spiritual life, perhaps even a greater one in our day than in Dante's, is a lack of fortitude or courage in the face of hard work or pain. The "soft pillows of down" Virgil describes so dismissively could symbolize so much in our lives. We have grown so accustomed to comfort and ease that we are used to employing only a small fraction of our power. We don't even *know* we have the power to do so much more. Working to the fullness of our strength is something very few have ever experienced. We can be so afraid of being tired or being in pain that we despair of the journey. But what do the fearful or slothful have

to show for their lives? Nothing more than "smoke in air or foam upon the sea" (51): a sad epitaph for those who are prevented from running the noble race for salvation because of lack of courage.

55   Virgil reminds Dante that they have a long way to go; they need to keep moving. This little pit hardly compares to the climb they have ahead of them—out from the center of the earth and up Mount Purgatory. Their journey is just beginning.

58   Dante has learned his lesson well. He refuses to let himself be governed merely by how he *feels* at the moment. He realizes that, right now, he needs to push ahead, and so he does. "Let's go, for I am bold and strong."

64   The imagery of Dante's not being able to speak quite normally because of being out of breath is immediately echoed by the voice he hears coming out of the next ditch: a voice "ill suited to form words." Dante can hear the voice but not make out what is being said.

70   In addition to the difficulty Dante has had hearing what is being said in this pit, he also cannot see. This ditch is characterized by extreme darkness. Dante, from his position at the top of the arch of the bridge over the pit, can make out nothing at the bottom. Here dwell those who are certainly children of the darkness or of the night. In fact, the sinners here seem to elude all of the senses. They move like thieves in the night,

for that is what they are, although Dante has yet to discover this.

Dante's eagerness to find out whom he has heard speaking and what is being punished in this pit overcomes his weariness. He asks Virgil whether they can climb down to the short side of the pit to investigate more closely. Virgil, especially after his earlier encouragement to shake off sluggishness, is only too happy to comply.

82 The pit is filled with an amazing assortment of snakes and serpents. The serpents call to mind the garden of Eden and might seem to symbolize sin in general, but no particular sin is immediately signified. Who are these sinners and for what sin are they being punished? Their identity is not revealed. That very fact, as we shall see, is itself revealing.

94 The first clue we have to what is going on here is the precise way in which some of the snakes attack the souls. Their wrists are bound by the snakes behind the sinners' backs and then immobilized against their backs. The souls are like handcuffed criminals, arrested by the police.

97 Next we are distracted by the sight of a sinner being bitten by a snake right at the nape of the neck. But rather than slowly being affected by poison, the man bursts into flames and disappears in a heap of ashes. If this isn't confusing enough, the heap immediately reforms itself and returns to its previous form, like a

phoenix rising from its ashes. He looks around himself, confused at what has happened to him. For what sin is this an appropriate punishment?

> It might seem strange that a religion that preaches detachment from material things also defends the basic human right to ownership of private property. Although we can easily fall into the temptation of placing our trust in material wealth, eliminating personal ownership would not solve the problem; in fact, it would cause an even greater one. If we are to have freedom to decide to live according to God's laws and our own conscience, we need to have some sort of financial independence. If someone else gives us all we need, that person can compel us to act merely by withholding what we need for life. As the old saying goes, "He who pays the piper calls the tune."

127 The soul who introduces himself to Dante as Vanni Fucci is famous as a man of violence and bloodshed. If that is true, then what is he doing down here instead of in the river Phlegethon in the circle of the violent? What people didn't know about him was that he was also a thief, not nearly as heroic-seeming as his more famous sins. When Fucci hears Dante's questioning, he blushes with shame, a shame at having been found out. *Being* a thief is not his disgrace—being *caught* is. His exposure, he says, causes him more pain than the death he endured: "It pains me that you've caught me

here / thrust in the misery where you see me now, / more than it pained me to be snatched from life." He was a thief, and disguise and darkness were the tools of his trade. For him, being caught was a failure.

Not only is Fucci's own cover blown. Now we know all of those who are being punished here: thieves. Now the earlier images begin to make sense. This trench of hell *should* be noted for its darkness, for these sinners worked "like a thief in the night." They did all they could to escape being seen or heard: their success depended upon it. Their appearance is obscured; even their voices seem disguised.

136 It also pains Fucci that it is not within his power to evade Dante's questions. He resents Dante for doing this to him and will find some way to get back at him.

151 In retaliation for having his cover blown by Dante, Fucci foretells the events that will lead to Dante's exile. He speaks merely out of vengeance: "I've told you this for spite, to bring you grief."

CANTO 25

Work as an Extension of Ourselves
Identity Theft

Christians believe that we work not out of mere necessity in order to sustain our families and ourselves as a sort of necessary evil. We work as an expression of our humanity, a display of our own kind of creativity. After all, we are made in the image of a God who is a creator. When you take away what I have produced, you take away part of me. What I have made, what I have worked for, is an extension of me. That is why we call it "property," what belongs, or is proper, to me.

1   It is striking that the thief is so violent in his opposition to God. We don't regularly think of sins against property as being so malicious. We might think that Fucci's rebellion against God is something peculiar to him personally, but Dante seems to have something more general in mind, something that ties the sin of

the thief to this violent anger towards God (see line 13 below).

4   Dante's sympathy for the souls in hell has often been an obstacle preventing him from deriving the full spiritual benefit intended from his journey. As Virgil frequently reminds him, pity isn't appropriate when souls are receiving the just consequence of their freely chosen actions. We are right to be horrified at the destructive power of sin; we can be saddened at the senseless waste of human life and potential. But pity implies we think the souls are "hard done by," and that is just wrong.

But here Dante does not struggle against misplaced pity. He is fed up with Fucci. The text suggests that Fucci's attitude towards God is what triggers Dante's strong reaction: "From that point on . . ." But it certainly seems possible that Dante is moved even more by Fucci's spiteful prophecy about Dante's own political party in Florence. Far from pitying Fucci, Dante says that the "snakes were friends to me." The serpents themselves seem to want to shut Fucci up (line 6), but certainly no more than Dante does.

13 Dante remarks that Fucci is the haughtiest soul against God in all of hell so far, even more so than Capaneus, the defiant blasphemer we met in canto 14. Why does a thief deserve this dubious honor? Dante obviously has something more in mind when he thinks of stealing than merely the alienation of someone's material

goods. In Dante's mind, stealing is a fraudulent version of violence against God.

Being a thief is a sort of rejection of work, or "human industry" as Dante called it. In canto 17, when he described the fate of the usurers, Dante had described this rejection of human industry as a sort of violence against God. See also the end of canto 11 (especially line 94 to the end) where Virgil explains the rationale for the organization of hell. The usurers rejected the nature God had bestowed upon them. To reject nature is to reject the source of that nature, our Creator, and work is built into our nature. That is why man was given the task of working *even in the garden of Eden*. Work was part of paradise. What changed after the fall was not the *fact* of work, but its burdensomeness. What we did before as a pleasure has become toilsome.

This human industry is a gift from God, part of our nature, a way we imitate God by sharing in his activity, his dominion over material creation. The thief is not only deceitful but also a violator of human industry. That helps to explain why Fucci seems to display so much anger towards God.

17 Even a centaur named Cacus shares in this serpentine fate. He, too, was a sneak thief, one done in by Hercules. Like Fucci, Cacus was also violent and murderous, but his thievery is considered worse, more destructive to his humanity. That is why this centaur is not punished with the others in the river of blood.

CANTO 25

> IDENTITY theft is a constant threat in our increasingly digital age. A business's website is compromised or our personal computer is hacked and suddenly our personal identification, our private numbers and passwords, are in someone else's hands. They can now pass themselves off as us.
>
> But all theft is an issue of identity: the hidden identity of the thief and the stolen identity of the victim. The distinction between what is mine and what is yours is violated.

40   This inability to recognize people here is an important theme. Identity, both hidden and lost, is a recurring image, central for understanding Dante's view of thievery. These sinners hid their own identity in order to commit their crimes undetected and stole the identity of others by stealing the private property of others. Hidden identity is part of the reason for the darkness of this particular pit: sneak thieves work under cover of darkness. Here they are condemned to the darkness that they willingly used to their advantage on earth.

In keeping with this spirit of secrecy, Dante learns the name of one of the sinners only accidentally. It was a slip on the sinner's part, naming names. Dante signals Virgil ("I laid my finger to my lips") to be quiet so that they can continue to eavesdrop on this conversation. Their covert listening is a way to break through the secrecy of this malebolgia. The thieves didn't respect the privacy of their victims; in a sort of retributive justice, they do not deserve that their privacy should be maintained here.

50   Dante gives a detailed account of what he now sees, in a scene reminiscent of Ovid's *Metamorphoses*. A serpent melds his identity with that of one of the souls. Neither nature is respected; neither remains intact. They melt together like wax, forming something that is neither serpent nor man. Neither is what (or who) he was before: "Each former countenance was canceled out; the image in perversion seemed both two and nothing" (76). This disrespect for a person's individual identity becomes an image of the sin punished here. Identity has been stolen from both the sinner and the victim.

55   The attack of the serpent upon the man is disturbingly intimate. The description almost sounds like a rape. With thievery, our privacy is violated. Someone else has rummaged through things that we intend no one else to see or touch, let alone take. This sense of invasion of what belongs to me, almost as much as the loss of the material things themselves, is the wound caused by the thief: there is a violation of privacy which feels strangely physical. We cannot think about our home in the same way. We cannot feel safe and comfortable there. Our domestic world is shattered by the intrusion of a thief.

79   Another bizarre transformation happens, but the mechanics of it are quite different from the first.

Instead of a blending of identities, here we see a sort of exchange. A small serpent bites a man at the navel and the two switch identities while Dante and Virgil watch. The description is a literary tour de force that lasts most of the rest of the canto, but is it anything more than an opportunity for Dante to measure his abilities against the descriptions of metamorphosis offered by Lucan and Ovid? It is difficult to assign meaning to these transformations since they seem to be happening in different ways each time.

But the precise metamorphosis is perhaps not so much the point. The focus of the imagery is that no one's identity is his own. It can be taken from him in any number of ways, ways that appear almost random, and there seems to be nothing he can do to stop it.

And why is this a fitting punishment for thievery? Private property is a divine right that enables us to be free to make our own decisions about how to live our lives. The right to life and the right to property are very closely associated, because property gives us the *means* to live. This was why both violence against life and violence against property were punished together in the river Phlegethon in canto 12. Our material goods truly *belong* to us. It is called *property* for good reason: it is proper to a person; it belongs to him and to him alone, and, in a sense, is part of his identity. This is partly why, when someone close to us dies, we want to have something that belonged to the deceased. It isn't just the material possession (at least not usually); it's that this thing *belonged* to the person we loved.

By taking another's property with no thought of its rightful owner, thieves reject the boundary between what is mine and what is yours, and, as a result, reject identity itself. This same lack of human respect that they displayed on earth is now their punishment. And so they have to watch as what belongs most intimately to them—their very appearance—is passed around from soul to soul in a macabre game of "keep-away." Here we have the hellish version of identity theft.

CANTO 26

The Solitary Path
Special Gifts and Special Responsibilities
Gifted Failures
Gifts as God's Investments in Us
Demagogues and True Leaders

In the spiritual life, we often depend upon support and guidance from the Church, friends, and family, or from good books, or the intercession of the saints. In the end, however, no one can do it for us, just as someone might help us rehabilitate after surgery but cannot exercise on our behalf. The spiritual life is something personal, something between us and God.

But when we think of drawing closer to God, the natural response to his infinite greatness is to become more aware of our own limitations and frailty. Standing in God's presence is a humbling experience. It is easy to wonder why God would even be interested in drawing us to himself. "What is man that you are mindful of him and the son of man that you care for him?" (Ps 8:4).

15 After inveighing against the evils of Florence, Dante scrambles up the bridge to the next ditch. His climb is an image of the spiritual life. He shows by his own example that the only way forward in the spiritual life is through humility and divine assistance. Dante needs Virgil's assistance to pull him up, and even with that help Dante needs to go down on all fours in order to manage to get to the top: "We couldn't move the foot without the hand."

Similarly, in our own lives, regardless of the assistance we receive along the way, we must choose in our own hearts to walk the path of the spiritual life; no one else can do it for us, though they can help. Perhaps that is what makes it a solitary way, regardless of the companionship of Virgil.

Here the way, the "solitary" way, is particularly treacherous. Perhaps this image is part of Dante's preparation for meeting the next group of sinners. We are entering into a pit in which people of great genius are being punished, not for having that genius, but for misusing it. The steepness of the way is an indication of how hard it can be to possess great gifts and talents and yet to remain humble and dedicated to the spiritual life.

21 The theme of humility continues. Dante must restrain his poetic talent here, holding his "genius under tighter

rein" (perhaps the greatest mortification for him), lest it dash off without the guidance of virtue. This is yet another example of Dante "front-loading" the imagery, subtly preparing the reader for what is to come before he explicitly raises the subject. Dante is preparing the way, by means of his imagery, for the hubris of the false counselors, who have used their genius at the service of vice. They are punished here for the abuse of the very power they share with Dante, a power he is now convinced must be placed under the guidance of virtue.

> "AND his gifts were that some should be apostles, some prophets, some evangelists, and some pastors and teachers, to equip the saints for the work of ministry" (Eph 4:11–12). We believe that God has endowed some people with special intellectual and rhetorical gifts, gifts to teach, advise, guide, and lead. But what happens when the light entrusted to them is misused? Their personal charisma and talents lead others falsely, like the candle that attracts the moth, only to destroy it. They will be responsible not only for their own failings but for those of the people who trustingly followed them.

25 The imagery in this ditch is focused on light—with particular reference to the scriptural image of the lamp on a lamp stand and the image of the city shining on a hill. The light, according to the scriptural metaphor, is

to be placed on high for all to see. The purpose of the light, after all, is to illuminate.

Here, however, the imagery is all inverted: the light is placed in the pit, down low rather than on high, and only flickering like fireflies. This light does not do what it was intended to do: shed useful light. The light illuminates only itself but nothing around it.

40 Until this point in the narrative, the imagery seems quite peaceful—as Dante himself says, like a warm summer evening—until the reality of this light is revealed. The light itself is fraudulent: what it is in reality is not what it appears to be. These flickering lights are not fireflies. They are damned souls; the sinful soul is the wick at the center of the flame: "Not one flickering light reveals the theft, / for each one stows away a sinner's soul." This light of the flame is fraudulent also in its function, because rather than illuminating in any useful way as flames normally do, here the light obscures their identities. The light itself, the symbol of their genius, has become their punishment, burning but not shedding helpful light. The reality that he observes is so strange that Dante still stares in wonder until he hears it from Virgil. He couldn't believe his own eyes, but Virgil gives him reassurance.

55 Ulysses and Diomedes are punished together because they sinned together. This is an important clue to the true sin of Ulysses: not the sin he so eloquently recounts later in the canto, but the sin he committed *with* Diomedes, namely the Trojan Horse: "As two they meet / God's vengeance, as they sinned and met His wrath" (56–57). Ulysses's account of his apparently heroic journey is a classic case of misdirection. His speech hides the truth rather than reveals it. Diomedes's presence reminds us of the truth of Ulysses's sin, even if Ulysses himself won't confess it openly to Dante and Vigil.

> HERO worship has a long and very human history. It is part of our nature to look to others for inspiration in our own lives. When we find someone who seems to embody our ideals and rise above normal human frailties, we hold them up as shining examples to be followed or imitated. And we expect them to live up to the picture we have formed of them by acting in an edifying and inspiring way. How disappointing it can be when we discover that our hero has clay feet! Their faults, now that we see them, appear even more severe than those of "normal" people, since we expect so much more of them; they had so much potential. As the old Latin saying goes, "corruptio optimi pessima," the corruption of the best is the worst. The failures of the rich and famous are obvious targets of our judgment. How could people who had been given so much fall so far? But each one of us will be judged not only about whether we have sinned but also about whether we have used our gifts profitably. Who can really say, "I have done all that I could do with what I have been given"?

65. Dante, as a poet, wants to meet Ulysses: "Teacher, I pray with all my heart, / and pray again up to a thousand prayers." The Trojan War is, for Dante, part of the foundational myth of the Holy Roman Empire: Aeneas flees Troy precisely so that Rome can be founded. Just as Dante was drawn to Homer in the circle of Limbo, so here he wants to converse with one of the characters from Homer's great works: Ulysses. But Virgil,

although granting Dante's request, requires Dante to be silent. His language would offend Ulysses's Greek ears—yet another humiliation for a man who makes his living by his words.

79 Virgil, whose epic *The Aeneid* continued the story begun by Homer, calls out to Diomedes and Ulysses almost as a suppliant. Throughout the journey with Dante, Virgil has commanded the damned souls to speak, but here it is only humble beseeching that comes from his mouth. That is the proper tone for true genius.

88 Speech seems to cause the flame to intensify. The act of communicating appears to add to the soul's sufferings. The flame moves with the words, as though the flame itself were the tongue speaking. Dante is refining the imagery of the flame. Now it seems to be a tongue of fire, like that which descended on Pentecost, bringing with it the gifts of the Holy Spirit. These souls, the false counselors like Ulysses or Guido da Montefeltro, had great gifts of communicating, a sort of secular gift of tongues. These might have been natural gifts, but they are gifts nonetheless, and gifts which carried with them a responsibility. This ditch of hell is, in a real way, about the *responsibility of genius*. The recipient of such gifts is supposed to become the servant of the talents entrusted to him.

> "Every one to whom much is given, of him will much be required" (Lk 12:48). Gifts and talents bring with them responsibilities. God expects a return upon the talents entrusted to us. These gifts were given to us by God. Although it is tempting to take credit for them ourselves or to use them for our own profit or glorification, they are not our exclusive property but rather God's investment in us. The Church reminds us of the source of our talents when we venerate the saints: "For you are praised in the company of your Saints and, in crowning their merits, you crown your own gifts" (Preface of the Saints I).

90   Ulysses's speech is one that must be greeted with great caution. We cannot take his words at face value, because speech has been the tool of his trade and his instrument of sin. Are we to hear a truthful assessment of his failures (a sort of confession) or are we to be treated to a display of his sinful technique? *Caveat auditor*—Listener beware.

As we listen to his explanation of the reason for his damnation, compare it to the facts. He sinned jointly with Diomedes. That is why he is here. But where is Diomedes in his account of his sea voyage? He seems to be using the classical device of misdirection, telling us a story that is compelling and entertaining but does not really respond directly to our questions. Are his words anything more than a cover-up for the ignoble trickery of the Trojan horse? Perhaps Ulysses does not want to be remembered for something that might appear to be a cowardly tactic: not the legacy a hero wants to leave behind him.

91 The sorceress Circe couldn't make Ulysses lay aside the love he had for his son, his father, and his wife, Penelope. He presents himself as a devoted family man struggling heroically against temptation. Nothing base could keep him away from his loved ones. He is leading the reader to the conclusion that something greater, something noble, would be the only thing that could turn him away.

98 Ulysses describes his journey as a noble quest for full human experience: ". . . to gain experience of the world, and learn of every human vice, and human worth." What some might consider irresponsible and even uncharitable towards his wife and family waiting for him at home, Ulysses casts as a noble enterprise. He intends to inspire his listeners by his words and example: nothing should stand in the way of our quests—we need to be ready to sacrifice lesser things for those truly noble goals that define the dignity of our humanity.

But is the desire to experience life to the fullest really the same as the noble desire for knowledge? Do we need experience of every vice in order to be wise? His words sound shockingly like those of the serpent in the Garden of Eden, leading Eve to experience Good and Evil firsthand, and so become like God. The original seducer was, after all, first an angel of light. Perhaps that helps explain why someone so far down in hell can come across as such an appealing and sympathetic character. And perhaps the fact of his appeal tells us something more about us than it does about him—that we are still susceptible to that original call of pride, to know things and do things for ourselves, without God.

106 The pillars of Hercules (the straits of Gibraltar) were the boundaries of the ancient world. Prudence would seem to demand that they stop there. Most moderns, however, would look on Ulysses's determination to continue as brave and heroic, a supremely human achievement, redefining our own limitations. Ulysses is moving beyond his own boundaries, "to boldly go where no man has gone before." Don't we all want to cheer him on? Doesn't real progress require that bold men like him make these choices, risk even their lives, and discover new things? Perhaps his boat should be christened the HMS Pelagian, after the heretic who argued that we could work out our salvation through our own power and initiative.

Ulysses is being bold if those boundaries and limitations are in fact false, and human capabilities can go beyond them. But are all boundaries false? Can we redefine ourselves *ad infinitum*? Our status as creatures, whether known through revelation or metaphysical analysis, tells us that we are, by our very nature, finite beings—that is precisely what it means to be a creature. Does our dignity come from redefining ourselves however we please and as frequently as we please or in discovering what God has created us to be? An existentialist would give a very different answer from that of a Christian. It is that existentialist inside all of us who cheers on Ulysses, but wasn't that same voice offering the apple to Eve, suggesting that she redefine herself, as the *Catechism* describes, ". . . without God, before God, and not in accordance with God" (CCC 398)? God both gives us our limitations and calls us to move beyond those obstacles that are placed in our path by sin or sociological influences. He comes to set us free.

> We seem to live in a world where a leader is considered great because he has the ability to stir up a crowd. But the ability to manipulate to action is not the same thing as leading. True leadership requires a clear sense of our ultimate goals and priorities and a wisdom about how to achieve those goals. Merely inciting a crowd might require skill, but it is the art of the demagogue not of the leader. History offers us many examples of this important distinction, but unfortunately those examples are most frequently of demagoguery rather than leadership.

119 Notice that Ulysses calls on his comrades to be real men. "For you were never made to live like brutes, but to pursue the good in mind and deed." His words so inflame them that "I hardly could have held them

after that." His words have done their job; his speech is "successful," if by that you mean that Ulysses has got his own way. His gifts have been used, he has won, and they will follow him. In justice, he must bear some responsibility for them, because they are with him only because of his ability, and his desire, to convince them.

But where is he leading them? What good are they pursuing? What truth are they hoping to discover? Isn't it really just the thrill of adventure dressed up in the garments of a noble quest?

133 It turns out that there is no new knowledge, no noble goal achieved. After five months of traveling, their only discovery is the sighting of a mountain that is tall beyond their wildest imagination. This mountain, in fact Mount Purgatory in the southern hemisphere, is a sign of the salvation that could have been theirs if they had been humble enough to submit themselves to God. Within sight of this symbol of God's ever-active mercy, of God's working to help them to overcome their self-imposed limitations, their boat sinks. There *are* boats that will make it to the shores of that mountain, but only those with God (or his representative) as the helmsman. God himself would have brought them to this very spot, to the shores of purgatory. We can't arrive there by our own devices. No adventurer will ever discover it. As Dante has shown by example, it is only discovered on one's knees.

CANTO 27

Words That Punish Us
Holding Our Tongue
Blame and Avoidance of Blame

In Aesop's fable "The Boy Who Cried Wolf," the boy's continual lying makes his fellow villagers no longer trust him. They had come running to his defense many times only to find that there was no wolf; it had all been a fabrication of his overactive imagination and desire for attention. But when a wolf actually threatens the boy, his cries bring no response from the wearied villagers. His words no longer carry any weight with them; he has lost their trust. His own words have come back to punish him. Lies and deceptions have a striking way of doing just that: they seem to exact their own revenge.

1   The flame that envelops the soul of Ulysses grows still when there is nothing left to be said. The activity of the flame is somehow connected with the activity of

the speaking. Speaking produces a greater intensity in the flame and, one supposes, a great suffering for the soul enclosed in it.

14 ". . . converted to the language of fire." The suicides were only able to speak when their limbs were broken for them. In life, they couldn't communicate their sufferings except by inflicting pain upon themselves. Their communication meant the shedding of blood—they could be said to speak the "language of blood."

As we continue in the ditch of the false counselors, we encounter a different sort of abuse of communication from that of the suicides. Instead of the language of blood, the souls in here are condemned to speak the "language of fire." These people had been masters of the art of communication while on earth but have now lost their natural voices. The fire must speak on their behalf. It is the motion of the tongue of fire, not of their own tongues, that produces the speech. Every word is produced only by the mediation of the fire. The parallel with the ancient story of the "Sicilian bull" makes the imagery even clearer. The red-hot bronze bull imprisoned its victim, and its specially crafted mouth became the channel through which its voice was transmitted to the outside.

This "language of fire" is an appropriate punishment for these sinners. The fire of truth has been entrusted to each soul made in the image of God, by virtue of our rationality, but in an especially abundant way to those gifted with a genius for words. If we don't use our speech to shed light, then the fire of truth will consume its speaker. The talent itself carries with it a risk, a built-in punishment for its abuse.

> WE feel the need to speak. Whether it is a matter of having our say, getting attention, participating in conversation, feeling important because we have information to divulge, or merely hearing the sound of our own voice, speech is something most people find difficult to control. Saint James identifies human speech as a source of many difficulties: "So the tongue is a little member and boasts of great things. How great a forest is set ablaze by a small fire! And the tongue is a fire. The tongue is an unrighteous world among our members, staining the whole body, setting on fire the cycle of nature, and set on fire by hell. For every kind of beast and bird, of reptile and sea creature, can be tamed and has been tamed by humankind, but no human being can tame the tongue" (Jas 3:5–8). When we speak in an unguarded way, we will end up regretting at least something that we revealed. Despite the repeated experience of regret, we still cannot control our tongue: the desire to speak, a desire that feels like a need, is too great.

22 Guido wants to speak to Dante, having heard the Lombard dialect being spoken. For these gifted speakers, the opportunity for conversation is too tempting to be passed up. He initiates the conversation at great personal cost, because the act of speaking intensifies

the flame in which he is engulfed. "You see it does not vex me—and I burn!"

28   We are reminded again that the damned souls might have special knowledge of the future, but the *present* is unknown to them. Dante is Guido's only source of current events. Why this strange inability to see the present? Because God, whom they have rejected, is the eternal present. What happens to these souls when time reaches its fulfillment? All they will have is their past, leading nowhere. Everyone who invests solely in temporal goods is doing the same thing—placing his heart upon things that are, in the final analysis, "dead ends."

61   Guido only speaks because he is convinced that what he says will never leave hell. Dante makes no move to correct him before he speaks. Is Dante's silence misleading? Is he being unfair to Guido? No. This is part of Guido's punishment. His speech, which got him into hell in the first place, now adds to his suffering. What Guido did was something hidden from view, but now his desire to speak has made his hidden infamy public knowledge, and we, centuries later, are still talking about him. His own speech brings this suffering upon him. He has no one to blame but himself. As Guido begins to talk, we need to remember that his speech, like that of Ulysses, is likely to be misleading. We need to be on guard to see the truth beneath his compellingly presented account.

> BLAMING others is as old as the human race. When God spoke to Adam in the Garden about why he had eaten of the forbidden fruit, Adam was quick with an explanation: the woman you gave me presented me with the apple and I ate it. The blame is clearly either Eve's or perhaps even God's! Eve uses the same technique but shifts the blame to the serpent. When we have done something that is obviously wrong, we feel the overwhelming need to edit the "narrative" to explain away what might seem to be our guilt. Usually this editing includes an attempt to shift the blame to others. We emphasize some elements and omit inconvenient details elsewhere (with the dedication and skill of a professional "spin doctor") to maintain our façade of innocence. No wonder Saint Philip Neri called people who made excuses or shifted the blame "Madonna Eva," Lady Eve. We prove ourselves to be the rightful heirs of Adam and Eve every time we cover our tracks and refuse to accept responsibility courageously.

70   Guido begins his story by blaming Pope Boniface VIII for drawing him back into his former faults. As in the case of Ulysses, are we hearing a balanced assessment of the facts, or Guido's own rationalization? In this ditch in particular, we must listen critically. We are in the presence of masters of avoiding responsibility.

100 Guido says that Pope Boniface offered him absolution in advance of the sin, something clearly impossible theologically since absolution requires contrition, and

contrition includes a firm purpose not to sin again. A plan to sin and a purpose of amendment cannot coexist. It sounds as though Guido is accusing Boniface himself of being a false counselor. Is Guido a victim rather than a sinner? Notice that the discussion is entirely about Boniface's counsel rather than about the advice Guido gave: a classic case of redirection. What was it that *he* counseled? About that, he is silent.

121   Guido might have fallen for Boniface's supposed absolution, but the demon sent to collect his soul at the time of his death did not. The demon knew that absolution and a decision to sin are mutually exclusive, violations of the principle of non-contradiction, which every student of philosophy should know. You cannot hold the same thing and its opposite at the same time. As the devil reminded Guido, "Perhaps you hadn't thought that I was a logician." Perhaps it's a good idea to take logic seriously, after all!

CANTO 28

Refusing to Give In
Humility and Believing
Us and Them
Sacrificing for Unity

It can be disturbing to watch people argue. They seem to hold on to their positions for dear life without ever entertaining the slightest doubt that they might be wrong. But how can they be so sure? And often, as an objective observer, we think to ourselves, "What difference does it really make?" The difference is our pride in being right. We are willing to fight for it, even when the cost is horribly high. We sow divisions with those around us by our words. Once spoken, they cannot be unsaid; once spoken, we are too proud to back down. These wounds can be very deep and are not easily healed.

1   Again, humility is the overriding image. Dante the poet is unable to put the scene into words. He needs to

admit his own limitations, in the very area that matters most to him. This humility had been lacking in the false counselors, but it is also absent from the souls we are about to meet. As we will see, their pride led them to break themselves and others away from the social and ecclesiastical unity that our humanity needs. They thought they were sufficient unto themselves: they would do things *their way*. His inability to describe what he sees also relates to the unnaturalness of what he is experiencing.

22 Here we meet the sinners sliced and wounded in such a variety of ways as to almost numb the mind and the emotions. Every conceivable sort of cutting seems represented. The descriptions are brutal, and even rather crass: "from the chin severed down to where we fart." This man's inner organs hang out of his wound, a sickening display depicted without any delicacy, with a sort of brutality of language. There is no suggestion of sympathy for their sufferings—only horror and disgust.

These divisions break the unity human beings are supposed to have with one another in three different ways: in the Mystical Body of Christ that is the Church, in civil government, and in the family. These bonds are presented in increasing order of importance. Ecclesiastical schism might seem to be the worst, but it is supernatural and founded in some way on the others. Political unity is more natural than the supernatural unity of the Church and therefore more fundamental, harder to get wrong. The unity of the family is the most natural: blood is thicker than water. Mohammed, Curio, and Bertran de Born will be the main representatives of each sort of breaking of bonds.

> THINKING about God requires a special sort of humility. Many of the truths we are considering are supernatural: they are beyond the capacity of our human intellects. We know they are true (and can know them with certainty) only because God himself has revealed them to us. It is on his authority that we accept them, not because we are able to grasp them with our own powers or verify them with our senses. That is why God institutes a Church that is divinely guided in its teachings. Only God can interpret God accurately! And so, if I am unsure about what a particular part of God's revelation means, I might make my own speculation, but I should only hold on to it until the divine authority has spoken. The same hesitation to cling to opinions is just as important to the professional theologian as to the everyday Christian. Once I know that truths are supernatural, to act as though I can know them by myself without God's assistance is fraudulent.

30   "See how I split the haunch!" He doesn't hide his suffering or the sin that caused it. He displays it for all to see.

　　Why the active voice rather than the passive that one would expect in the circumstances? He himself is split, but his wounds are a sort of incarnation of his sin—they display the destruction he has wrought by his own actions. Dante calls this the law of counter-penalty. This punishment is not merely a punishment but a distillation of the sin itself. This man, Mohammed, as it turns out, can honestly say, "See how *I* split the haunch!"

Why is Mohammed here among the schismatics?

St. John Damascene, familiar with Islam and its origins, lists Islam as a Christian heresy. Perhaps because of his influence, in the Middle Ages, Mohammed was viewed as a Christian schismatic or heretic. By Dante's time, Mohammed had become a sort of "poster boy" for schism, threatening and dividing Christendom on both religious and political grounds. If Christendom was to be destroyed, Christians thought that it was Islam through which this destruction would occur. The Church is, at Dante's time, fighting back the Moors in Spain, a process that will go on until the Battle of Grenada in 1492, and Islamic power in the East is threatening ancient Christian communities. This is the age of Crusades, an attempt to reunite ancient Christendom; Islam was seen as the great obstacle to that unity.

Ali is Mohammed's son-in-law. His later break from Mohammed's path would become the source of the division between Sunni and Shi'a Muslims. The imagery of Ali's wound is intended to show that the destruction Mohammed had begun, Ali completed. Mohammed was cut from his chin all the way through his body. Ali is cut from the top of his head to the chin. Together, they represent a completely severed person, cut entirely in half.

Dante is, I think, making Mohammed a sort of personification of division, rather than considering him as a true historical figure. The result is a caricature of schism, not a true picture of the way even medieval intellectuals would have viewed Muslims. Dante would have been well aware of the Dominicans' great attempt to learn more about and enter into dialogue with followers of Islam. Dante, for example, places both the great Arab philosophers Avicenna and Averroes (despite their being Muslim) in limbo, with Aristotle, not here with Mohammed. This is not a blanket rejection of all followers of Islam, but rather a rejection of those who caused the original break, again bearing in mind Damascene's view of Islam as a Christian heresy.

34   Mohammed now explains precisely *what* these souls have split; he is the spokesman for the whole collection of sowers of discord. He explains that they are sowers of "scandal, discord, [and] schism." They have split the body politic, the family, and the Mystical Body of Christ. These "bodies" are more than mere metaphors. The bonds they represent are essential to the fulfillment of man's nature and supernatural destiny. Man, the social animal, cannot exist without these bonds. As Donne, said, "no man is an island." And so, those who cause these bonds to be cut asunder inflict untold damage.

37   The souls are sliced by a devil as they process around the circumference of this circle of hell, calling to mind a cruel imitation of a penitential procession. Just when they are healing, they reach the devil again and their wounds are reopened. This suggests the ongoing nature of their sin. Schisms are not the work of a day—they require perseverance in malice. There is

a *determination* about their sin, a consistent plan of attack.

46   Virgil speaks with a sort of respect to Mohammed. He answers his question truthfully and straightforwardly.

52   The souls seem more amazed at Dante than he is at them, amazed that he has the possibility of returning to the land of the living. But unlike the other souls, who wanted news of friends or relatives, or wanted messages sent back, Mohammed, displaying his own division from humanity, only seems eager to send back a cruel taunt to a relatively unknown heretic known as Fra Dolcin. There is no fellow feeling here, just a sort of mocking irony, rubbing it in. His lack of concern for his followers on earth is a final display of the broken bonds he has caused.

> WE seem to live in an age of intensifying polarization in politics. The lines between "us and them" are clearly drawn and do not seem likely to shift anytime soon. Politicians speak the language of inclusivity and finding common ground but end up hurling divisive slogans aimed at energizing the party faithful. Early Christians were commanded to pray for the emperor and to serve their nation well. "First of all, then, I urge that supplications, prayers, intercessions, and thanksgivings be made for all men, for kings and all who are in high positions, that we may lead a quiet and peaceable life, godly and respectful in every way. This is good and it is acceptable

> in the sight of God our Savior" (1 Tm 2:1–3). Christians were not allowed to turn even their pagan rulers into "them." We are even told to love our enemies. "You have heard that it was said, 'You shall love your neighbor and hate your enemy.' But I say to you, Love your enemies and pray for those who persecute you" (Mt 5:43–44). For Christians, there are only two sorts of people in the world: those who are already our brothers and sisters in Christ and those who are supposed to be. We are not given the luxury of writing people off.

64 Those who were involved in schism seem to be afflicted with vertical cuts, reminding us that these supernatural bonds are supposed to be aids in our moving towards our supernatural destiny with God in heaven. Those who are sowers of political or familial discord seem to have horizontal cuts. The bonds they broke were intended to tie us with our fellow man in a more earthly fashion. We are now moving into those who sowed political discord.

70 Pier da Medicina seems to speak from much the same motive as Mohammed did. He is stirring up trouble, causing division, even from beyond the grave. His prophecies are motivated by malice.

96 Curio's advice broke the political alliance, and even the bond by marriage, between Caesar and Pompey. For that wicked advice, his tongue is split down to its root. We discover this only because his companion

forces open his mouth and reveals his disgrace. There is no loyalty here. Discord is still being sown among the damned souls. Curio seems stricken and downcast by this treatment, which is the natural consequence of breaking down ties of trust. The man without hands shows the same dismay—"he went away as one beset with gloom / and madness."

We cannot live without social bonds. By severing them, these souls have undermined their happiness, and even their sanity. We can't be fully human if we are "cut off."

> WHERE there is the deepest connection, there is also the possibility of the deepest wound. No one can hurt us like family can. With them we are simultaneously more vulnerable because our own weaknesses are known, and we are less guarded with our words. Horrible things get said, things we would not say to anyone else. It is almost shocking how much must be forgiven if family life is to succeed. Too often, however, these vindictive words cause wounds that seem incurable and unforgivable, producing what the divorce courts call "irreconcilable differences." Every human bond, even one so fundamental and natural as the bond of family, demands special care and sacrifice if it is to survive. And without these bonds, we will not survive.

118 A headless man, carrying his own head like a lantern, appears. It would be interesting to examine each of

these sowers of discord and see how their particular sins correspond with the precise wound inflicted by the devil. We can guess that he somehow divided the body from its head.

124 "He made himself a lamp unto himself." These words recall the false counselors, who used their talents to

deceive rather than illuminate the path for others. A similar reality is at work here but with greater malice. Here the deception isn't merely about getting one's own way. It is even more sinister as its goal is the destruction of all human ties. This man has followed his own way rather than considering the common good.

The imagery becomes particularly shocking when he raises up the head high to get closer to Dante standing on the bridge over the ditch. If we find the human body so divided to be shocking, then how should we view society or a family or the Church cut off from its head?

133 Bertran de Born encouraged a son against his father, a subject against his king: a double break in one act. He recognizes the fittingness of his punishment. "Because I severed two such persons joined, / severed I carry now my brains, alas, / from their stem in this trunk. Thus you may see / the rule of retribution work in me."

CANTO 29

Hardness of Heart Is Easy
Family Bonds and Family Feuds
The Trust That Binds Together Society
Lack of Empathy and Lack of Manners

When we contemplate the infinite mercy of God, we should be filled with hope that reaching the promised reward of heaven is possible; our many sins and failures will not stand in the way of God's forgiveness. And the hope we have for our own salvation is a hope we extend to each and every human soul: may God's mercy touch them and move them to conversion. But God's openness to us and our openness to him are two different things. Religion is often ridiculed, and God is either ignored or rejected as a crutch for feeble minds. Perhaps the hardness we have all observed (and probably felt at times in our own hearts) makes Our Lord's warning more comprehensible: "Enter by the narrow gate; for the gate is wide and the way is easy, that leads to destruction, and those who enter by it are many" (Mt 7:13).

CANTO 29

1   Dante is moved to tears. "I longed to stay a little while and weep." Were we wrong in saying that disgust, rather than sympathy, was his reaction to this ditch of sinners? Virgil notices and questions him—these displays of sorrow have no place when seeing the just punishment of the damned. Virgil has corrected Dante's sentimentality before; he thought that issue had been resolved.

9   Even though we have descended so far into the pit of hell, the circumference (smaller in each circle) is still twenty-two miles here. Unfortunately, hell needs to be so vast as this—to accommodate all those who refuse happiness.

> FAMILY strife has an impressive staying power. It is a frequent but unfortunate part of our "inheritance" that we grow up with divisions and controversies as a normal part of life. There are people to whom we do not speak or businesses we do not patronize. Families have long memories. Maintaining peace and connection within our families and with our neighbors is a beautiful and valuable heirloom to pass on to our descendants.

13 Dante thinks that Virgil doesn't understand him: "If you had paid attention to the cause, / . . . you might have granted me a longer pause" (13, 15). He thinks he is being corrected again for having sympathy for the damned. That is not the issue here. Dante explains his

tears: among the damned souls, he spotted a relative of his, Geri del Bello.

But Virgil already knows and understands. He noticed more than Dante thought he did. He saw the soul pointing Dante out to the others and uttering threats. Del Bello is upset because his relative Dante has not avenged him. Dante is struggling with his own anger and resentment at what he considers the unjust fate of his family and the exile he currently endures. The threats of his relative are the last straw.

Virgil advises him to forget all about him. Injustice can be addressed, but vengeance (so much a part of Italian society then, and sadly still with us today) is not the way. Del Bello is a personal witness to that, even though his words say the contrary. We can see in him where the "code of honor" has got him. Vengeance is not the road to justice but to hell. Dante sees that if he yields to his thoughts of revenge, he could very well join Geri in this pit. He could become an instrument of the division he witnesses so graphically.

Dante weeps in part because of the sorrow of seeing his own relative suffer, partly from the frustration that bearing injustice has laid upon his spirit, but in part, at least we can hope, because he sees the horrible destination at the end of the road he himself has been traveling. We can see these different motives for tears in Dante's words to Virgil: "I think a spirit of my own blood mourns / the wickedness that down there costs so much" (20–21).

22 Virgil's objective eye sees so much more than Dante, overwhelmed as he is with his own emotional reactions to what he sees. "Your mind was then so seized . . ." (28). When we are struggling under intense emotions, we focus so much on the source of our struggle that we develop a sort of tunnel vision. We don't see things we would otherwise notice, and we misinterpret what we do see. Dante is so overwhelmed by Bertran de Born that he doesn't notice Geri at first. And in the midst of that turmoil, he misinterprets Virgil's words to him.

This is a lesson in our own need for an objective eye when we are fighting against strong emotions. We need someone to listen, not in order to agree with us, but in order to correct our perspective, as Virgil does for Dante here. This might be a spiritual director or even a wise friend, someone to see what we do not see.

39 Again darkness is the first thing we notice about this, the final malebolgia. Darkness and fraud naturally go together. This will not end up being the main image associated with this sin, but it is the first to come to Dante's attention. It is, in a way, the genus or general category of fraud. Later we will encounter the image that sets this sin apart from other sins of fraud.

45 Dante struggles not to be drawn into sympathy for the damned souls. Their cries, like the siren's song we heard about in Ulysses's account of his sea voyage, are overwhelming, resisted only by blocking his ears. Ulysses had to lash himself to the mast to keep from being drawn in by the siren's song.

> A body begins to rot when the parts that used to work as a unity begin to fall apart; they decompose. The same thing happens in society. When the bonds that hold us together no longer function, communities fall apart; they rot. When we smell the rot in our own world, we must remember that only true connection will counteract the decomposition.

50   In this final ditch of this circle, the dominant, defining, and even overwhelming image is the stench: the souls smell like they are rotting—"as comes from members dying of the rot" (51). What sin could this smell of decay signify?

57   Strangely enough, in this deepest ditch of the circle of simple fraud, we come across something that might seem petty, at least compared with what we have already seen—counterfeiting or falsifying. But, as we have learned several times, Dante (and God, too, Dante would want us to know) takes sins against property very seriously, since personal property is our means of personal sustenance and a guarantee of some measure of freedom in our lives. For reasons we shall see, counterfeiting is worse than all the other sins against property we have seen punished higher up in hell.

60   Again the smell is the major image. The air is so "pestilential" that it would make any living thing drop dead. The sin we are about to encounter not only stinks but this stink has the power to wipe out life as we know it.

It undermines everything. It is the smell of the death of society.

67. We are given another clue to the true nature of this sin: the souls are sprawled out without regard for one another. It is as though they don't even recognize one another's presence. Here we see an outward sign of the

ultimate breakdown in human solidarity and society: living in one another's physical presence but entirely isolated from any meaningful interaction. To complete the imagery in a modern way, perhaps the souls should be listening to iPods. Modern cities can be disturbingly like this final ditch, with people traveling together on mass transit without so much as eye contact, let alone anything like conversation.

75. As a final clue, and to complete the imagery of decay, the skin of these souls is covered with scabs. They are breaking down, and as they scratch themselves, little bits and pieces of themselves go flying, as when a fisherman scales a large fish. Perhaps these also symbolize the way these counterfeiters alienated the property of others. Some have suggested that the scales they scatter look like coins and are as valuable as the debased money they brought into circulation.

> ONCE we feel unconnected with the people around us and our empathy is gone, quickly the outward show of connection disappears. Simple manners are an embodiment of connection. Without human connection, there are no manners. Without manners, society must produce detailed rules for everything. The good works that might flow naturally from being connected with others are now considered foreign and quaint. In a proper world, who would need a sign to tell him to give up his seat for an elderly or handicapped person? Such things should not need to be said. But we now find a need to say them. That is a very bad sign.

85 Virgil speaks to these sinners with a sort of dismissive sarcasm. Even when they answer his questions, he responds by wishing them eternal fingernails that will allow them to scratch forever.

97 All the souls who hear that Virgil is guiding the living Dante through hell immediately react to him, turning towards him and trembling. What is the cause of this reaction? They seemed lost in their own little worlds until Dante and Virgil appeared. Their physical presence wasn't enough to excite their interest. It is only when Virgil explains the mission he is on that they snap to attention.

103 Dante takes up Virgil's tone. Don't let "your tedious and repulsive pains" get in the way of telling me who you are. Why the scorn?

109 Gruffolino was a famous alchemist. The story he tells about his execution for suspicion of heresy does not account for his being *here* in hell. After clearing his name regarding the heresy, he admits that alchemy is the reason for his damnation.

The focus of most alchemists was turning lead into gold, a tempting project since lead was inexpensive and yet so similar to gold in its properties, as we saw in the circle of the hypocrites. The chemicals used in their attempts to bring about this very profitable transformation often caused horrible skin irritations. These chemicals are perhaps part of the reason for the leprosy-like disease from which they suffer.

139 "How fine an ape of Nature's works I was." By counterfeiting, and doing a respectably good job about it, these souls were able to pass off their fake coins for the real thing. This flood of fake money undermined not only the economy of the cities but, even more importantly, the *trust* between citizens needed in society. When the means of exchange (money) is called into question, how can normal trade and transactions continue? When currencies crash, people can't buy what they need with the pay they received for the labor. When people won't accept money because it might be fake, the money we have becomes useless for providing for our needs. That makes the labor that earned that money useless. We have worked for nothing. Those who receive a fake coin and pass it on unknowingly end up being implicated in fraud themselves.

We depend upon one another in a complex society for the necessities of life. We are not self-sufficient farmers, producing everything we consume. We work, get paid, and use our wages to buy what we ourselves do not produce. This specialization is an important prerequisite for culture, our freedom to give our energies to things which are not strictly essential. But how can we get what we need if no one trusts the money we try to use to buy it? Without a stable economy (which requires a stable currency), human society breaks down, the fabric of our daily life unravels, and civilization decays.

CANTO 30

Individuality as God's Gift, Not Our Decision
Sin as the Ultimate Reality Show

The modern world treats an individual's identity as though it were something fluid, a matter of design or choice. Who we are as a person is supposedly a blank slate upon which we can inscribe whatever we desire. But the Church teaches us that we do not construct our identities: we discover them. Our task in the spiritual life is to purify and strengthen who we are. When a raw jewel is mined, it looks to the untrained observer much like other jewels. Only when it is cleaned up does its nature begin to show itself. But its full beauty is revealed only when the jewel is cut and faceted. Then it begins to sparkle with its greatest glory. The process of growing in holiness is not a matter of forcing individuals into a pre-set mold, eliminating everything that makes them distinct. Holiness respects individuality completely. Others might try to steal our identity, but God never will. Our individuality is his gift to us. We are the ones most likely to reject that individuality by constructing a false self.

4   We are now about to meet a new group of sinners in this final ditch of the circle of the fraudulent—falsifiers of a different sort—imposters, counterfeiters of human identity. Although thieves were said to steal their victim's identity by taking their property, imposters take the identity itself.

After meeting the falsifiers of money, we are presented with the image of King Athamas and then Queen Hecuba of Troy. The king becomes so crazed that he forgets his own identity, killing one of his sons and causing the death of the other and their mother. It is not merely the brutality of his attack that is important here. Hecuba loses her mind, ". . . howling like a dog, / so badly her grief twisted her mind" (20–21). This being "beside oneself" is the real point. It is another example of Dante introducing a topic indirectly, through the imagery employed.

31 Perhaps the trembling that Dante and Virgil noticed was arising from the dog-eat-dog atmosphere of the circle. There is a tone of madness, of the breakdown of rationality and civility. Who can be peaceful, or even fully human, living like that?

32 Gianni Schicchi, a clever imposter, attacks his fellow sinners like a wild boar. His viciousness, as described by Dante, is starkly contrasted with Puccini's gentle treatment of the same character in his opera *Gianni*

Schicchi. Puccini treats Schicchi's story as a comedy of mistaken identity, a man who impersonates another in order to falsify a will, but all for a good cause, for the financial well-being of a pair of young lovers. We're meant to see Gianni as a clever sneak, the sort of rule-breaker who isn't entirely to be trusted, but whom you might like to have on your side in a tricky situation.

Dante obviously views it in a more serious way, placing Schicchi deep in hell. The breakdown of society caused by the breakdown in trust through counterfeiting and impersonation results in the suppression of what is truly human and leaves behind only the bestial drives to rule—a sort of Darwinian survival of the fittest. Human society is not supposed to be "nature red in tooth and claw," but the dissolution of trust can quickly make it just that. Schicchi is, in Dante's view, the embodiment of that descent to the level of the beast.

37   Notice that Myrrha is also an adulteress, but she is punished as a counterfeiter not as an adulteress. The deception (which is a perversion of her uniquely human power of reason) is more corruptive of human good than the disordered sexuality she displays.

Again, we are reminded that, according to Dante, a sin is greater which produces a greater harm, not to our neighbor, or to God (which isn't really possible anyway, since God cannot be harmed or even changed), but to our own human nature. We offend God by destroying that creature made in his image, a

creature whom he loves—ourselves. That is why sins of reason are graver than sins of passion: because they corrupt something more fundamental in us, something at the very core of what it means to be human. From another point of view, reason can work to bring disordered passions back into order. So long as we have reason, we have the possibility of reform. But once reason is disordered, what can put it back on track? To use a scriptural image, "You are the salt of the earth; but if salt has lost its taste, how shall its saltiness be restored?" (Mt 5:13). We are intended to be creatures guided by "right reason;" reason is our salt.

Even more than our private material goods, our personal identity and appearance belong to us—they are our property. So one who impersonates is therefore a thief. Compare these sinners with the thieves in cantos 24 and 25, whose identities are stolen from them since they did not respect what belonged to others.

52   The man's dropsy "distorts his limbs," making him almost unrecognizable. His true identity is obscured. He is trapped in a body that barely seems his own, entombed in flesh. Master Adam was a counterfeiter who debased the pure gold florin for profit. It seems fitting that his punishment involves a terrible thirst, like the rich man in the Gospel parable. He thirsted after the wrong things in life, and now he thirsts continuously and will never be satisfied.

64   Imagining what he cannot have only increases Master Adam's pain. The rushing water of the streams "are ever before me" (67), tantalizing him with an object beyond his reach. The desire of his eyes for what wasn't really his was the cause of his sin in the world and continues to increase his suffering even now.

76   Master Adam longs to see his fellow sinners condemned—one has been already—but he could not go

to see them in their misery, for his limbs were bound. If he could drag himself an inch a century to see them suffer, he would. He'd even willingly trade the opportunity to drink at a fountain in order to see them suffer. No fellow feeling or empathy is left—no desire for their conversion or hope that they might escape a fate so cruel as his own. In this he is different from the rich man in the Gospel parable who is surprised to find himself in hell. That man wanted a messenger to go back to earth to warn his brothers so that they wouldn't suffer the same fate that he had.

> THERE is a strange and rather sleazy delight we take in observing other people, and especially when they are acting badly. Reality shows and live streaming help feed this fascination for the modern world, but it has always been around. In the past, it was gossip columns and peep shows, but the delight was the same—looking from an unseen viewing post at something that should be private. It is the thrill of the voyeur, the Peeping Tom. It grabs our attention and holds on to it. We are mesmerized by what we see, almost addicted to it. But what does it do to us? Our imaginations are filled with salacious images; we have become people who watch life rather than people who live it for themselves.

94 Two sinners, who have been there since Master Adam arrived but without moving, are steaming and stinking with a pestilential fever. When Adam identifies

them and their crimes, one, Sinon of Troy, arises from his feverous stupor and attacks him—". . . banged with his fist that swollen bag of guts." The violence becomes reciprocal, and both physical and verbal. Their exchange fascinates in an illicit sort of way, like watching some talk shows on daytime television. The key imagery here is the total breakdown of human connection. This decay of the bonds that united one human being with another is the direct result of the failure of trust brought about by the falsification these sinners have committed. What they experience here in hell is what they helped bring about in their own societies while on earth.

130 Dante succumbs to the fascination of this sparring match with a sort of prurient interest. Virgil quickly reprimands him: "You keep looking there and in a while *I'll* pick a fight with *you*" (131–32). Dante is immediately stunned by the anger in Virgil's voice. Virgil is deadly serious about what he is saying. He casts aside Dante's embarrassment, assuring him that his contrition itself is enough to remove his guilt. But he leaves him with this stern reminder that is even more fitting in our own age, with the media so ready to supply the information (and the pictures) to satisfy all of our vain curiosity—"To want to hear it is a base desire" (148).

Curiosity is not the same as the noble desire for the truth. Dante came to hell to learn about the sins that condemned people to an eternity of suffering. He is here precisely in order to gather information about hell, information intended to help him change his life. But Dante had already learned what he needed to know in this ditch without indulging in the juicy details of this verbal battle. How often we allow that "base desire" to rule us in our conversations, wanting to know what we have no business knowing, knowledge that contributes to nothing but our own inflated sense of our self-importance—placing ourselves at the judge's bench ("the arbiter," in Virgil's words), viewing the mess of people's lives, their weaknesses and failures, from atop our pedestal of supposed objectivity.

CANTO 31

The Power of Silence
Perspective and Experience in the Spiritual Life
Natural Gifts and Supernatural Glory

Robert Cardinal Sarah, in his recent book *The Power of Silence: Against the Dictatorship of Noise*, argues that interior silence is a foundation of the spiritual life. Interior silence requires at least some attempt at exterior silence, blocking out the noise from entering our minds, like astronomers who head out into the desert to escape the light pollution that will interfere with their observation of the stars. Our minds are overstimulated by being perpetually bombarded by images and sounds. And like a small child suffering from ADHD, we often can find it hard to focus, hard to filter out the constant chatter. If we are to lift our minds and hearts to God, we need to escape the background noise and rediscover the power of silence.

8   The images of speech and listening set the tone for

the beginning of this canto. As we prepare to descend into the pit of hell, we are given time to reflect, along with Dante, on what Saint Paul calls the "smallest of members," the tongue, which is also the most difficult to control. Whether we are involved in conversations actively (by speaking) or passively (by listening attentively), we are still accountable for it. Dante erred by his avid listening to the mudslinging of Master Adam and Sinon of Troy. By participating, even passively, in their conversation, he too is tarnished by it. As the ditches of fraud have taught us in many different ways, communication is a powerful thing—and therefore also a dangerous thing, to be used carefully. Perhaps this is *part* of the reason so many spiritual guides encourage silence and so many religious have times of enforced silence in their daily schedule. Here Virgil and Dante walk on "with no more conversation."

10 Here nothing is quite what it seems to be, as in those deceptive moments at twilight when we can easily mistake what we think we see. In all fraud, appearances are deceiving. The intention is to build up a "false front" that will take in the observer.

> IN the spiritual life, what you see is not what you get. Temptations come in alluring disguises, which should not be surprising since the devil is the father of lies. Making good choices about decisive moments in our lives requires careful discernment over time best done in silence. Often we plunge ahead impulsively before we

can even see clearly. When we cannot see for ourselves, we need the guidance of someone with a fuller perspective and greater experience.

12   Despite the twilight that makes seeing very difficult, the sound of the trumpet's blast comes through like a foghorn, louder than the loudest thunder. But even this loud signal is deceptive. When Roland blew his horn at the battle of Roncesvalles, as Dante reminds us, the signal was clear: the enemy's army was no longer retreating but had turned and was now attacking. Roland's signal alerted his troops and saved the day.

But what does the blast on the trumpet mean here? Is a battle about to be waged? Is some danger approaching? What does it signify? It is deceptive not because it is weak and difficult to sense (like visual images at twilight) but because the signal itself, clear and loud as a sound, could be interpreted in different ways by the hearer. The sound is clear, but its meaning is not.

19   Dante's apparent vision of towers ("or so it seemed") adds another layer to the deception. He thinks he is entering a fortified city, but Virgil warns him of his mistaken conclusion: "Imagination tangles you in knots." The reality, as is often the case with fraud, is worse than it seems, and Virgil knows he needs to prepare Dante so that he won't be terrified by the shock.

28   Virgil ends his warning by taking Dante "by the hand

affectionately," another sign intended to soothe Dante's fears and prepare him for the reality he will soon discover. What Dante thought to be towers are in fact enormous giants, standing in the pit of hell, but towering over the rim of the pit. They might seem like towers from where Dante observes them, but they are even larger than they seem: he only sees them from the navel up.

As is the case with fraud, what we actually see of the giants is the least of our worries, merely the tip of the iceberg. When the full reality of the giants becomes clearer to Dante as he approached them, "my errors fled from me and my fear grew" (39). The full truth sometimes does not make things easier but more frightening. Many patients dread learning their diagnosis from their doctor. Knowing will force us to face the truth, and that moment of reckoning will challenge our courage.

44   Here we find the giants and titans, another example of Dante's blending together Scripture and mythology, but there is a reason for their being together. What both have in common is their attempt to challenge God (or the gods) on their own terms—a refusal to accept their creaturely status. Dante, following a patristic tradition, associated the builders of the Tower of Babel with Nimrod and with the Nephilim, the race of giants described in Genesis 6:4. In this account, the giants tried to build the Tower of Babel in order to reach heaven, the ultimate challenge to the authority

of the transcendent God. The titans are recorded as trying much the same thing against Mount Olympus and the Greek gods.

And so it seems fitting that these rebellious brutes should stand watch over the depths of hell, where Satan, who made the original refusal to serve God, is forever entombed. These giants are the guards of the inner "sanctum" of the city of Dis, the devil's "Swiss Guards."

55 Dante sees the wiping out of the giants as an act of mercy by God. Such strength should not be allowed to be united with the power of the intellect. There is simply too much potential for evil in such creatures.

> NATURAL gifts are impressive, at least at first glance. When the Prophet Samuel was sent to anoint one of Jesse's sons as king, he was immediately struck by Eliab, the eldest; this must be the one, he thought. "But the Lord said to Samuel, 'Do not look on his appearance or on the height of his stature, because I have rejected him; for the Lord sees not as man sees'" (1 Sm 16:7). When natural gifts are not directed to their proper end, what started off as impressive can become rather pathetic. How the great have fallen.

67 Nimrod speaks gibberish to us, at least as far as anyone can tell—fitting for the someone responsible for the Tower of Babel. His attempt to build a tower that would reach the heavens, punished by the shattering

of the unity of human language, is the ultimate stupidity—no one can be like God, except those to whom God gives that likeness as a *gift*. Rightly does Virgil call him "stupid soul!" (In my childhood, calling someone a "Nimrod" was a fairly standard playground insult.)

The stupidity of his attempt to conquer God is now mirrored by his inability to communicate. No one understands anything he says, and he understands nothing that anyone says to him. His communication, loud though it is, doesn't *signify*. He babbles and blows his horn (randomly, it seems), but he isn't bright enough even to *find* the horn that is strapped across his chest: "Feel round your neck and there you'll find the strap / that keeps it tied, O spirit of confusion — / and see it make the stripe across your chest." This inability to communicate is an image of the ultimate stupidity of challenging God and will be a recurring theme for the rest of the *Inferno*, reaching its fullness in the person of Satan. How the mighty have fallen!

79 Virgil has no respect for Nimrod. He even appears to taunt him. In the end, Nimrod is not worth wasting words on: "Let's leave him and not toss our words away." There is nothing heroic here, nothing impressive except size. He is worthy of ridicule. He is pathetic.

94 Here again we find Dante blending together classical imagery with Scripture. The titan Ephialtes is a classical version of Nimrod. He tried to climb Mount Olympus and conquer the Gods. He is now immobilized by powerful chains. The hands he lifted up in rebellion against the gods will never be lifted again.

100 Antaeus is chosen as the giant who will lower them into the pit of hell. He was killed by Hercules but lived too late to take part in the rebellion against the gods. That is why he is unchained and has some limited ability to speak. The pride, however, which characterizes

his fellow giants and titans is definitely present in Antaeus, and Virgil uses it to manipulate him into doing his bidding.

106 Ephialtes shakes like an earthquake when Virgil mentions that Briareus looks "more ferocious" than he does. His titanic pride has been insulted. His pride

makes him an easy target of manipulation. It makes him weak.

112 Antaeus and the other giants and titans do form a sort of inner guard for the citadel of hell. Hell is a sort of anti-heavenly city. Here those gathered around the throne do not bow down in worship and sing praises. They are immobile, mute, and stupid. The "city" of Satan is being guarded by fools.

115 Virgil flatters Antaeus, recalling his greatness, and promises that Dante will make his greatness known when he returns to life on earth. Because of his pride, his desire for lasting fame in the world above, Antaeus, one of the inner guards of hell, ends up being God's instrument, assisting Virgil and Dante on their journey. So much for their strength and ferocity! Antaeus gives into their request "in haste" (130), especially when Virgil suggests that they might ask someone else (Typhon or Tityus). He is eager, and even performs his task with gentleness, setting them softly at the bottom of the pit.

CANTO 32

The Gradual Freezing of Love
The Enduring Power of Hate
The Pain of Betrayal
As Good as Our Word

Exactly how and when a heart hardens seems almost mysterious, but the reality is obvious: we reach a point of no return, a place at which our heart no longer can be melted by kind words, tender memories, or a generous action. Something has died inside. The heart can become petrified or frozen, and when this happens, it seems frighteningly inhuman, and the actions that flow from it are almost incomprehensible. How could a person even think of doing that? Because something inside has died. But it dies one small act of bitterness and unforgiveness at a time. Freezing rarely happens in an instant.

1   Here the evil is beyond the power of expression, even for someone of Dante's literary talents, because it is beyond human comprehension. The things that we

consider the most important, the noblest, are precisely what are rejected here; the bonds which are the closest to our hearts have been willingly broken by these sinners. Such treachery leaves even Dante speechless. It would do the same to anyone who "calls 'mama' and 'dada'" because anyone who has done so, anyone who has known the love of parents, knows by experience the depths of these personal connections. What evil is needed to tear us away from those closest to us? How is this a choice worth making in the minds of these sinners? Because it *is* a choice they made. Dante, suffering the pains of exile, finds it difficult to imagine for himself, and, as a result, difficult to put into convincing poetry. As has been so often the case, the imagery of the sins punished here actually precedes the experience, preparing the reader for what he is about to encounter.

10   True malice, evil done wholeheartedly, is almost mysterious. We are left to face this same mystery when we ask ourselves how Adam and Eve, content in their paradise, could possibly have chosen to rebel against God. The question is even more perplexing when we ask it about the angels in heaven who joined Satan in the great rebellion. Shouldn't they know better? Shouldn't they know that God is their true happiness and what they are pursuing will make them miserable, both now and forever? What could lead a being with such special knowledge, with such special grace, free from all taint of sin, to choose something evil? There are few questions in theology more difficult than this one. That is

why Dante calls on the Muses to inspire him. Figuring out this puzzle will require supernatural guidance.

15 Ancient thinkers held it as a truth that the corruption of the best is the worst. It is better to have been created a lesser being, to have been given less, than to have been given so much and lost it. These souls appear to have abandoned all that makes human beings human, all that sets us apart from the beasts. These words also call to mind Our Lord's words when he speaks about someone leading astray one of his little ones: "It would be better for him to have a great millstone fastened round his neck and to be drowned in the depth of the sea" (Mt 18:6).

16 As in the beginning of canto 31, Dante doesn't recognize what he's getting into. He is still staring back at the giants lined up against the wall of the deep pit into which he has been set. He walks distractedly from where Antaeus put them down and is startled by a voice coming from an unexpected direction—at his feet. The words turn his attention downward, where he first notices that he is walking on a lake of ice, smooth as glass, but seemingly very strong, not fragile or brittle. Although he hears the words, he does not immediately place the voice of the one speaking. He reveals the exact location of the speaker only later.

31 The full horror of this canto comes as a surprise. Dante first describes to the reader the voice he hears, then the ice he sees, and finally, in an almost teasing fashion, reveals the fate of the sinners punished here. Again, he begins with an image rather than merely with a stated

fact. Like frogs in a pond, with their snouts sticking out of the water (the mention of the peasant girl only extends the suspense), the damned souls are frozen in the lake up to their necks.

34 Their suffering is almost ridiculed, treated as something less-than-human: their chattering teeth are like the clacking of storks' bills. Their teeth are chattering with the cold. The reference to being "livid grey, fixed in the ice up to where shame appears" reminds us that these treacherous souls could do the most outrageous evil without blushing; they were shameless while on earth. Now the cold takes away the color that would provide even the appearance of shame.

37 "Each held his face down low." This suggests some sort of shame, but we'll come to see that it is part of the hiddenness of fraud. They never let their true face be seen.

38 "Every eye / testified to the sorrow in the heart." Their tears are evident, because of the cold; as soon as they are shed, they freeze.

> No one is more attentive than a lover: except perhaps a hater. Human beings can hate with an intensity of focus that can become obsessive. Hatred in our heart drives us to the object we hate and binds us to it with a horrible tenacity. Love might fade, but hate seems to live on. Can we afford to give room in our hearts to something so destructive and controlling? "Do not let the sun go down on your anger, and give no opportunity to the devil" (Eph 4:26–27).

40   We see two sinners locked in a parody of a loving embrace: they are so close that their chests are pressed together and their hair has grown into one snarled mass. They have the outward appearance, and only the outward appearance, of unity. They have rejected the human bonds that they appear to represent.

46   Here their tears, tears of self-pity and frustration rather than of repentance, form part of their punishment. They freeze, locking the eyelids in place, impeding the sight of the sinners. They were blinded just as truly by their selfishness on earth, blinded even to the bonds of blood and kinship. Here their tears of self-pity serve as instruments of their punishment.

> It is painful to be let down by others. Everyone hopes to receive understanding and basic compassion from other people, even those whom we have never met, whether they be police officers, or bank tellers, or tax collectors. But when we do not experience this fellow feeling from those closest to us, that is more shocking and hurtful. As the Psalmist wrote, "It is not an enemy who taunts me—then I could bear it; it is not an adversary who deals insolently with me—then I could hide from him. But it is you, my equal, my companion, my familiar friend" (Ps 55:12–13). This sort of treachery shakes the very foundation of our world, leaving us exposed and alone. The human race has had to live face-to-face with such treachery since Cain slew his brother Abel.

49 Whatever doubts we might have had about these two souls and their apparent unity, whatever pity we might have felt for their tears, quickly disappears because of their head-butting. These are two brothers, each responsible for the other's death. Here they are doomed to be in each other's company for eternity. Their ties of blood, which ought to bring them consolation, bring only rage. It is fitting that this ring, the ring of traitors against family, fraud against the double bond of humanity and family relation, should be named after Cain, who instituted the sin of treachery against his own flesh and blood by the murder of his brother Abel.

54 "What mirror are you staring at in us?" The treacherous soul asks Dante why he is staring. Perhaps there is also the suggestion that Dante looks at the suffering souls but sees himself reflected in them. The souls must think that Dante could only be there in this circle of hell if he too had been condemned for treachery.

55 The first soul to speak to Dante here, a soul who had lost his ears to frostbite, remains anonymous himself initially, but he is only too ready to "rat out" the two souls locked in the embrace. He'll name names. There is no fellow feeling or sympathy among the souls condemned here. He is ready to make all the others seem worse than he is. To avoid further questioning from Dante, the soul identifies himself as Camiscion de' Pazzi.

70 Only now does Dante seem to be aware of the huge number of souls here. What he sees at his feet is not unique, but only one of a thousand examples of treachery. He'll never be able to look at a frozen lake in the same way again.

73 Dante uses both fire and ice in his description of hell. Ice might be an unexpected punishment for those accustomed to the more traditional hellfire, but the cold here in the place of treachery, however, seems particularly appropriate. All human warmth was extinguished in these hearts long ago, even towards those who should have been most likely to inspire them with love and affection, their family and friends.

Treachery is also not the sin of a moment. It is the result of resentment cultivated, grievance nurtured, or schemes plotted over time. A passionate man might decide upon his plan in a fit of rage but might also be turned away from his course of action. The treacherous man, on the other hand, is immovable in his decision. Nothing is allowed to stand in his way. His will is as permanent and unshifting as ice.

The sins that *are* punished with fire are of a very different sort—usually sins involving the passions. The sins punished here are not sins *motivated* by passion. They are committed with a certain "cold-bloodedness" that makes sins of passion appear far more understandable, far more human.

The poet Robert Frost, in his famous little poem

"Fire and Ice," artfully presents both sides of the debate over imagery for hell:

> Some say the world will end in fire,
> Some say in ice.
> From what I've tasted of desire
> I hold with those who favor fire.
> But if it had to perish twice,
> I think I know enough of hate
> To know that for destruction ice
> Is also great
> And would suffice.

> THERE is an old saying of unknown origin, "You are only as good as your word." What we say and what we promise matters among social beings. In our richly interconnected human world, many of our links with others are ones we enter into voluntarily. We pledge our loyalty to another, we make alliances to fight for each other, we join together into cities and nations. We often speak of these as being a matter of "social contract," but every contract is ultimately the result of a choice. If these agreements freely formed mean nothing, then where are we?

76   As he walks with Virgil, Dante kicks the face of soul stuck in the ice. He is quite coy about how exactly it happened: "If it was fortune, destiny, or will, / who knows." One might think Dante himself would! But he leaves us to decide the matter for ourselves. Is it more than a coincidence that this man betrayed

Dante's party in battle? He certainly leaves open the possibility that he kicked him intentionally.

Here we have entered Antenora (named after a Trojan traitor), the second circle of the final ring, where traitors against country are punished. Dante places traitors against country lower in hell than traitors against their own families. Why? The bond of family is more natural, more deeply seated, but the bond of party, nation, or country is freely entered into. As the saying goes, "you can't choose your family." To violate a bond freely entered into is a greater offense against our rational nature and more malicious than violating a bond over which we have no control.

81 "Why this injury?" Regardless of the betrayals this soul has committed against his own country, he still expects to be treated fairly by others. Bocca shows all the self-centeredness of the treacherous: the good of others can be sacrificed for his own advancement. He breaks the rules, even the most basic rules, but still expects others to play by them.

91 "But I'm alive." Dante tries the same tactic he has used (successfully) so often: he promises to make sure the memory of this soul continues on earth. But here such an offer isn't welcome. "I crave the opposite. . . . You don't know how to flatter for this pit." Here the rules are different. Traitors know they will receive no thanks for their actions, no pity for their sufferings. They want to disappear, to remain anonymous.

But Dante continues his prying for information and won't allow the sinner any privacy. He will make sure that he is exposed and his name recorded. Resorting to physical violence yet again, Dante yanks out clumps of the sinner's hair but elicits no response from him. Silence matters more than suffering. This desire to remain unnamed or anonymous, and not any shame they might feel for their crime, might explain why these souls have their heads bowed to the ice.

106 It is one of Bocca's fellow sinners who reveals his name just after clumps of his hair have been pulled out by Dante. It seems obvious that he does it out of malice. Bocca immediately reveals the identity of the soul who named him, fighting back with the only weapon he has—stripping him of his anonymity. And once the malice begins to flow, he identifies many others, even though they had done him no wrong. The insulted thug turns stool-pigeon—no loyalty, no pity for others, merely spite. Lack of loyalty was part of his sin, and this defect remains forever reflected in this soul. Should we expect anything different from someone so malicious against his own people?

124 Moving on, we are yet again shocked by the imagery before we get the details. Dante sees two men frozen in the same hole, the one gnawing the head of the other: "so did he gnaw the brains, the flesh, the skull." Dante is as intrigued as we are. Again, he offers the opportunity for the story to be told, but he has learned an

important lesson—revealing the evil of the enemy is more important to the one he is addressing than keeping alive his own memory. Tell me, Dante says, what your story is, and I will tell the world just how horrible your enemy truly is! Spite, not clearing one's own name, is what motivates here.

CANTO 33

Desensitizing Power of Sin
Climbing Into Our Own Little Pit

We like to think of ourselves as people with standards. There are certain things we simply would not do. But life often shows us, in a painful and often humiliating way, just how easily we can abandon those standards: the teenager committed to chastity who gives in to the sexual demands of her boyfriend in order to keep him, the good student who experiments with drugs in order to fit in with "friends" at a new school. But when our hearts become habituated in sin, the pressure to set aside our principles is not external: it comes from our very selves. A man goes to the casino for the entertainment and the inexpensive food but quickly becomes addicted to gambling. Soon he is missing work. Money is discovered missing at the store where he works. His children find their bank accounts empty. What has happened to this "good" man? His life seems to have gone down the drain, sucked under as by a whirlpool. But the difference between the gambler and the drowning man is that the one drowning is struggling against what is happening to him, flailing with his arms and legs to save himself, but the addicted gambler does not think there is anything from which he needs to be saved. Being oblivious to the danger is the most dangerous thing of all. There is no telling how low we will be dragged if we hold onto our sins.

2   The scene is horribly dehumanized. The "eater" wipes his mouth on the hair of the "eaten," displaying his utter disdain for him. His victim is lacking in dignity, worth nothing except as food. His treatment of his fellow sinner is reminiscent of those crimes of hatred in which the victim is disfigured or degraded. Somehow merely killing the victim does not seem to satisfy the hatred of the attacker. The victim's dignity and humanity must be stripped away as well.

7   Despite the pain of recalling the events that led him to hell, this soul willingly endures it for the sake of revenge. Although the souls in upper hell wanted to be remembered on earth as a sort of immortality, here in the realm of fraud, exposure is a punishment. Telling someone's story only brings shame. And so we see the souls being reticent about themselves but willing to tell all about their neighbors.

   This soul's vehemence should make the reader wary—such tortured souls, hungry for revenge, make notoriously unreliable witnesses. Self-justification and vengeance are powerful desires that trample over the truth.

16 Notice that Ugolino speaks of *Ruggieri's* "malicious plots" but makes no mention of why he himself is punished in the circle. Ugolino must be here for a reason, and the only possible reason, given the justice of the punishments of hell, is that he too is a traitor against his country. But he places the focus on Archbishop Ruggieri's guilt rather than his own. This misdirection is a classic technique for hiding one's own secret while appearing to be entirely open with the listener.

19 Ugolino admits what he cannot plausibly deny—those truths that are a matter of public record. Dante and his readers would be familiar enough with the general lines of the story. About what happened in the secrecy of his prison, however, no one can question his account of things. He and his sons were the only witnesses. Ugolino, it seems, will have the last word. There is no one who can contradict him.

37 Ugolino had been imprisoned with his sons by Ruggieri. That is merely an historical fact. It is unclear whether it is Dante or Ugolino himself who alters the story to make Ugolino's sons to be children ("my small sons"): they were grown men. This bit of information alters the entire tone of the story. Ugolino wasn't cruelly thrown into the tower with his little boys, but with his grown sons who were likely coconspirators, not innocent victims of Ruggieri's vindictiveness.

46 After months ("the passing moon several times over," line 26), already weakened by hunger and their imprisonment, waiting for food to be brought to them at the customary time, Ugolino and his sons hear instead the sounds of the tower door being nailed shut. They are being left to starve.

Ugolino says that he is beyond grief. His heart is turned to stone, frozen. But is it frozen with *compassion* for his sons or with *hatred* for Ruggieri? Ugolino does not tell us. The reader is left to assume or to draw the natural conclusion that paternal love is the reason his heart hardens. But the facts seem to indicate that Ugolino is absorbed in his own pain. He admits that he "spoke no more," but his silence seems to be the brooding silence of a man quietly nursing resentment and plotting revenge.

52 Ugolino's son Anselm pleads with his father, asking what is wrong. "Therefore I did not weep": he presents his lack of tears as a *response* to his son Anselm's plea, something he does to spare his son further suffering, but his lack of tears *precedes* the request. He does not *stop* weeping; he never started. It must, therefore, be for another reason. How could it be charitable to respond to the pleading of your son with no reply at all? How would that lessen his pain? What father would do that? Wouldn't a father say whatever he could to encourage and console his sons, to let them know, in his final hours, that he loves them? To remain silent for an entire day in the presence of the suffering

of those you love is an act of terrible emotional withdrawal. The reader is left to wonder whether this is really about their pain or his resentment. I think what Dante intends the reader to conclude is clear: Ugolino is so absorbed in himself and his resentments that he has abandoned his bond with his sons.

58 When Ugolino's sons see him biting his hands (the action immediately reminds the reader of his angry gnawing on the skull of Ruggieri), his sons are moved by compassion to act. They try to comfort him with their words and even with their own lives. Remember the story of the mother pelican, pecking her own breast to offer her blood as food for her offspring, which becomes a metaphor for Christ offering us his body and blood for our spiritual nourishment. Locked in a room together and facing death by starvation, it is the children who offer the father their own flesh for food. He gave them bodily life at the start; they are willing to return the gift. "You clothed us with / this wretched flesh, now strip it off again" (62–63). Dante uses this offer of themselves as food to prepare the reader to interpret Ugolino's final words in line 75 properly.

> THOSE who have had loved ones suffer from dementia often talk about their experience in terms of bereavement; it feels as though they have already lost them. How challenging and painful emotionally to sit beside a parent but to feel he or she is not there for you, not

> responsive to your needs or interested in your life. Their very presence makes that emotional distance feel greater. Sin can act much like dementia. The self-centeredness of our sins can distance us from those we love, shrouding us in our own little world. What pain have we caused them by our distractedness or distance?

64 But even this moving display of love and self-sacrifice from his sons elicits no response from Ugolino, only more silence. He withdraws even further, if that were possible. For the next two days, nothing is said, no words of encouragement or signs of affection are given. His heart must already truly be frozen to remain untouched by their words, but somehow his silence seems fitting for one whose sin is the breaking of special human bonds. The natural desire to support one another seems to have been driven out by Ugolino's private thoughts. The ice seems to have entered his heart even before he entered the frozen pit of Antenora.

67 Ugolino, having gone blind in his prison cell (another symbol of his separation from others), has to endure the pleading of his sons as they die of hunger in his presence over the next few days. They die without even hearing their father's voice or feeling his embrace. We can wonder whether his son Gaddo is hurt more by the hunger or by being abandoned emotionally by his father. "Papa, why don't you help me?" Gaddo, like his brothers, has been left alone to suffer in isolation. The

broken bond between sons and their father is a suffering imposed not only by Ruggieri but also by Ugolino himself.

72 Only when they are dead does Ugolino touch them, when they can no longer be consoled. His contact with them is about *his* suffering, not theirs. He had no pity but self-pity.

75 Ugolino's final words are horrifyingly vague: "Then hunger did what sorrow could not do." What did hunger do to him? The interpretation Ugolino wants to leave in our minds is that hunger killed him when you would have thought he would have died of sorrow first.

Perhaps he finally broke his self-absorbed silence. Did hunger break down his emotional reserve and allow him truly to grieve? This would seem only human, perhaps too human for someone so absorbed as Ugolino. The text gives us no evidence of such a softening of heart.

Perhaps, most distressingly, hunger drove him to abandon what little was left of any real fellow feeling, any respect for another person as fully human. Is this an admission of cannibalism? What his words might leave open to interpretation, his actions make clear: he concludes his story by beginning to gnaw on the skull of Ruggieri again. What Ruggieri had made Ugolino do to his sons, Ruggieri, in turn, now has done to him. He is now the eaten one. Is his punishment of gnawing Ruggieri a way of exposing his sin so that Dante can see it and report it? Was Anselm's offer of himself as food for his father a foreshadowing of what was to happen?

87   The cross of his sons was both hunger and the human separation their father's silence imposed upon them. Notice how the destructive effects of betrayal are felt in this life, not only by the sinners themselves, but by those around them.

We do not really know whether Ugolino's sons were party to his betrayal of his country. As adult sons, they might very well have conspired with their father. The testimony of the fraudulent cannot be taken at face value.

91   We pass to a third area, where the damned souls are even more incapacitated by the ice. Their heads are tipped backwards, filling their eye sockets with tears, which immediately turn to ice. This freezing over of their eyes denies them even the release that tears can bring and the freedom to give expression to their suffering: "Weeping itself forbids the souls to weep."

104 Dante feels a breeze, which is more than a disturbance of the air. The breeze is, as we will see in greater detail later, the source of the freezing in hell.

115 Dante shows no hesitation to deceive this soul by means of mental reservation in order to get him to tell his story: "If I don't clear your eyes, may I / go to the bottom of this icy Hell!" Dante knows perfectly well

that the pit of hell is exactly where he is headed. It seems only fair to trick the fraudulent.

118   Brother Alberigo, whom we meet here in the region of hell called Ptolomea, is somehow worse than the traitors we have met above, somehow deserving of being deeper in hell. In one sense, betraying one's family seems worse than betraying strangers, more unnatural. But the key here, however, is that it is worse to betray a bond into which one entered with full freedom. One cannot choose one's family, but one has some sort of control over one's nationality or party affiliation.

With Brother Alberigo, we see the betrayal of the freest of these three bonds, the bond of hospitality. Hospitality is a trademark of man's social nature, and the outward sign of the universal brotherhood of man. To choose to enter into the host/guest relationship voluntarily and then to cause harm to one's guests is to reject one's own dignity, one's connection with his fellow human beings. What is left of your humanity if your word, and your protection, freely offered, mean nothing? *Macbeth* offers us perhaps the greatest example of this sin in literature—Macbeth and his wife betray not only their king but also their house guest. The murder of Duncan is the source of the disintegration of the sanity of Macbeth and his wife. They abandoned their hold on what it means to be human.

121   "Are you dead already then?" Dante knows of Alberigo. When Dante left the world, Alberigo, to the best of

Dante's knowledge, was still alive. How can he be talking to him here in hell then?

The answer to this confusion on Dante's part is that betrayers of guests have a unique punishment in keeping with their rejection of the special bond of hospitality—their souls can go to hell while their bodies continue to move about on earth. A demon takes over the body until the time comes for it to die. The bond of body and soul refuses to coexist with such a profound violation of human connection. What appears to be a human life is no longer human; humanity has been sacrificed.

This strange punishment helps to emphasize the destructive power of malice. When our hearts get so frozen that there is no sympathy for our brothers and sisters and neighbors, we are dead spiritually already, whether we know it or not.

149 Alberigo has rejected human connection. He has violated his own solemn obligations. Why should he expect Dante to play by the rules where *he* is concerned? If Alberigo wants a life without connection, let him have it. "To be villainous to him was a courtesy." Notice that Dante uses the language of hospitality and graciousness: "a courtesy."

CANTO 34

The Overwhelming Emptiness of Evil
The Futility of Rebellion
Self-Inflicted Punishment
The Disappointing Spectacle of Evil
The Inescapable Providence of God
The Imprisoning Burden of Sin

Explaining the existence of evil was one of the great philosophical challenges. If everything that exists is somehow good, then what is evil? Evil must not be a "something" but an absence of good, technically a privation. Physical evil or suffering is perhaps the easiest to picture. The blind man suffers because he is missing something human beings expect to have: vision. Blindness is an absence of a good that should be present. Moral evil is the absence of the good that comes from our actions being ordered to reason. The more profound the evil, the greater the lack.

As we approach evil in its purest form, we are encountering not a great and powerful being but an overwhelming absence. If God in his goodness is the fullness of being, evil is emptiness.

1   We enter the pit of hell, Judecca (called so after Judas), accompanied by an almost liturgical note, with Virgil reciting a parody of the *Vexilla regis*, a hymn for Holy Week. We thus return to the idea of hell as an inversion of the City of God, a sort of anti-heaven. The giants and titans are like the angels who worship God in heaven. The frozen lake reminds us of the saints casting their crowns down upon the glassy sea (as in the hymn "Holy, holy, holy," referring to Rv 15:2). And whereas heaven is filled with songs of praise, hell is relatively silent, turned in upon itself and barren. This direct contrast between hell and heaven will continue throughout the canto.

4   We are in the depths of the region of the fraudulent. One of Dante's recurring themes in this part of hell is that nothing is quite what it seems to be. Remember the giants and titans at the edge of the pit of hell, whom Dante thought were towers. Now he sees what appears to be an enormous windmill and tries to hide from the frigid wind it produces. Regardless of what it is that Dante sees, the cold it produces is overwhelming, symbolizing a complete lack of love but also, to use the imagery of science, a lack of activity. Heat comes from motion. God is pure activity ("second act" in precise philosophical terms). By turning away from God, those who chose evil are left frozen,

static, unmoving, unchanging. The only vague sign of life turns out to be the almost automatic motion that produces the frigid wind.

10   The punishment here is more complete than in the previous rings—here is punished the sin of betraying a benefactor, literally someone who has acted well towards us, and as a result someone to whom we owe a debt of gratitude. The sin is therefore a double one—both betrayal and ingratitude, a rejection of the good actions of others towards us.

This most extreme example of the freezing of the human heart is punished by the souls being entirely encased in the ice. They are embedded in the pavement. They are entirely without movement. We cannot converse with them but only observe them as we would look at some inanimate object.

13   The souls seem to have been cast into the ice randomly—some are upright, others lying flat, others upside down, still others bent in half. They are like garbage that has been frozen in water, stuck wherever it landed. They have thrown away what made them human, and now they are tossed into the pit of hell, a sort of human litter.

20   "Behold there, Dis!" Hell, like heaven, is a *personal* reality, according to Dante. Heaven is heaven because of *who* is there, because of the vision of God. He makes heaven what it is. It isn't a perfect place, but rather a relationship between the soul and God, the relationship

that defines the rational creature's existence and happiness. We are blessed in heaven *because* we see God. We become like him, for we see him as he is.

At the core of hell is Satan—Dis, the rejecter of God who is the source of all bliss. Hell is hell not because of *where* it is, but because of *whom* it rejected. It is hell because God is missing; the absence of the Infinite Good is the greatest absence of all. Satan has been intruded in his place. But God is the only good that can satisfy the longing of our hearts. Without him, we are left unfulfilled, aching for more. Without the possibility of seeing him, we have no chance of happiness or human completeness. That is why the gates of hell (as seen in canto 3) tell all who approach them: "Abandon all hope you who enter here."

> BOETHIUS was thrown in prison by the emperor he had served, Theodoric. While awaiting his execution, he had the opportunity to contemplate what seemed to be a great act of injustice, of the abuse of power by someone in authority. But Boethius argued for a very different, and perhaps unexpected, conclusion: evil is powerless. All human beings desire happiness, and happiness is attained only by acting virtuously. Evil people want happiness but can never achieve it. "The wicked busy themselves with what gives pleasure without being able to achieve their real objective."[4] They might seem to be

---

[4] *The Consolation of Philosophy*, Book 4, prose 2; tr. Victor Watts, Penguin Books, 1999, p. 92.

> in charge, but they are in fact condemned to perpetual frustration. They can never get what they most deeply desire—that is powerlessness.

28   Satan is both enormous (he even dwarfs the giants), but also surprisingly powerless. He is trapped in the ice up to his waist, immobilized. We are reminded of the impressive stature of Satan as a creature. He was created to be something great and splendid. God showered him with unthinkable gifts. But because of his rebellion, his beauty as an angel of light (Lucifer) has been lost: "He was as fair as he is ugly now" (34). What an amazing loss!

37   Satan, who wanted to be like God, is a monstrous parody of the Trinity—three faces on one head. This is yet another instance of hell being the inversion of heaven.

> ONE of the spiritual maxims Saint Philip Neri would repeat to his disciples was, "Men are generally the carpenters of their own crosses" (28 March). We might imagine that our sufferings are inflicted by an unfeeling universe or a vengeful God, but a large number of them are self-inflicted. Part of the reason a loving God delivers commandments is that he knows (far better than we will in this life) that acting in certain ways will produce pain and suffering. Out of love for us, he intervenes to help prevent that pain. When we refuse to let go of the sin, the pain remains with us, the side-effect of our twisted choice.

46   Satan retains the triple set of angelic wings described by the prophets, enormous but hideous. Nothing is left of their angelic glory except their size; they are like the wings of bats—black and scaly. The flapping of these wings is what turns the water of the rivers of hell that flow into the pit into ice. Satan, therefore, is imprisoned precisely because of his own actions. God doesn't inflict this ice upon Satan. Satan produces it himself. He is his own jailer. The flapping of his wings freezes the ice that traps him, but nevertheless he continues to flap. His actions produce his sufferings, but still he cannot stop.

    It is part of Satan's punishment, perhaps the most painful part, that his plans are constantly frustrated. Regardless of what he sets out to do, the opposite happens. No matter how much he tries to rebel or stand in the way of God's plan, he only succeeds in being an instrument of God's will, and also an instrument of his own damnation. He is a horrible reminder of the way in which our own sins trap us in our own unhappiness, limiting our freedom and defacing our beauty. We are the architects of so many of our sufferings, but even when we realize this, we seem unable to change. We too can feel stuck, just as firmly as he is.

MILTON'S Satan is one of the great characters in literature: powerful, compelling, and undeniably attractive. His speech rallying the fallen angels in the first book of *Paradise Lost* is riveting; it is hard to imagine not being

> moved by it. He is a powerful and defiant arch-fiend, the ultimate villain that action movies and comic books try to replicate. He has a plan for world dominance; he is ready for battle.
>
> But perhaps Milton's picture of Satan tells us more about the power of evil in our world than about his personal state. What is really left of an angel of light once he has rejected the Light who made him? How much of his angelic splendor would survive his fall from heaven?

53 If Dante's reader were waiting for the great encounter with Satan, expecting lively debate and a show of power, the actual meeting would be an enormous disappointment. Here Satan is not glorious or interesting. He is viewed in his full emptiness and stupidity. Seen face-to-face, he is repulsive. He weeps and chews and drools and flaps. It seems mechanical, mindless, and endlessly dull—quite an anti-climax to Dante's dramatic journey.

How different this is from the vision of God with which the blessed souls are rewarded! In God are infinite riches, infinite truth. We can gaze for all of time and never exhaust the supply. He is infinitely interesting. The vision we have of him transforms us, lifts us up, makes us like him. Experiencing that vision, we can desire nothing else, because there is nothing else that is desirable that isn't included in God. He is all.

But Satan isn't remotely interesting or satisfying. We don't get to talk with him any more than we were able to talk to the souls embedded in the ice. He is too far gone. Dante rightly passes over him rather quickly, giving him far less attention than many of the sinners we met above. The further down we get, the less there is to see, because we get closer and closer to nothingness. We are reminded that sin is ultimately empty, boring, foolish, and unsatisfying. As Virgil will tell Dante in a few lines, "It's time to leave, / for Hell has nothing more for us to see" (68–69).

55 God gave himself for us to eat, his flesh for our salvation. His gift of himself in the Eucharist is an outward and visible sign of the infinite love God has for his creatures and of the lengths to which he will go to save us. He was willing to give himself for our sake.

Satan, on the contrary, consumes his minions, grinding them with his teeth. Even though they did his work on earth, they receive no gratitude, no reward—they have received their reward on earth. They betrayed their benefactors; why should they expect anything better from the one they served? If the chewing were not bad enough, his claws flay their flesh, calling to mind the scourging of Our Lord at the pillar.

61 The three sinners in the mouth of Satan betrayed not just any benefactor, but *the* benefactor, God himself, who has given to each creature all that it has, even its very being. Both Cassius and Brutus betrayed God by betraying Caesar, who, as emperor, was God's instrument on earth. Judas is the worst of the three because

he betrayed God Incarnate, not merely his earthly representative. Perhaps that is why he alone is headfirst in Satan's mouth.

> IN the movie *The Passion of the Christ,* Satan howls when he realizes that his conspiring to bring about the death of Our Lord has in fact resulted in the price being paid for our salvation. All of his work to destroy God's plan has only served to achieve it. One simply *cannot* rebel against an all-powerful God. No creature can stand outside of God's influence. We have power only insofar as it flows to us from him. That is what being a creature means. That is why his will is always done.

70   Virgil *uses* Satan. Timing the flapping of Satan's wings (they seem to be flapping automatically), Virgil treats Satan as a ladder, climbing down his matted, clumped, and frozen fur. Satan, yet again, despite his own intentions, becomes an instrument of God's plan and Dante's salvation. It seems to be Satan's worst punishment—the more he attempts to thwart God's will, the more he serves to bring it about.

76   Dante becomes bewildered when Virgil turns around and begins to go up. Dante thinks that they are returning to hell, but in fact they have merely passed the center of the earth, the point to which all gravity tends. To go further "down" requires one to go up. Dante begins to understand as they arrive at an opening in the rock,

a sort of cavern, and see Satan's legs sticking up into the air. They are now in the southern hemisphere.

98 "... a cavern nature carved." They will follow a passageway carved out by flowing water over the centuries. The river that eroded this rock and poured into the pit of hell will be identified only later.

121 They are now ascending to the opposite side of the earth from the point at which they entered hell. Satan's being cast out of heaven to earth has left an "impact crater" which is the pit of hell. The material displaced has been pushed to the opposite side of the earth, forming an enormous mountain in the southern hemisphere, the mountain that Ulysses was in sight of when his ship went down, Mount Purgatory. In other words, Satan's fall not only formed hell, but also purgatory, by which souls can ascend towards heaven. Satan again is acting as an instrument of salvation. As St. Paul said, "All things co-operate unto good."

128 It is dark. It is sound that guides them, the sound of a small stream. This stream, as we shall discover in *Purgatorio*, is the last of the four rivers of the classical underworld, the river Lethe. At the top of purgatory, the souls of the just wash in this river, cleansing them of the burden of their sins and hurts. The river drains away the pain and the remembrance of pain and empties into hell.

Following this stream, a stream of forgetfulness and forgiveness, Dante and Virgil make their way to the surface. How would we have the courage to make such a climb without the continual assurance of God's assistance and forgiveness? Even when we cannot see our way, God's forgiveness provides hope and direction, the promise of new life.

> FREEDOM: for those who are imprisoned, hospitalized, immobilized by infirmity, or held hostage by tyranny, there can be no sweeter word, no greater promise. We dream of being freed from our burdens, and there is no greater burden than the yoke of sin. Some of the great joys in beginning to live a spiritual life seriously are the little victories we achieve over long-standing habits. Each victory, though small in itself, is a taste of freedom, a glimpse of the way life can be. It promises us that we are not condemned to live with these burdens forever. There is a way out of the darkness. ". . . and you will know the truth, and the truth will make you free" (Jn 8:32).

135 Hearing the sound of the stream, realizing that they are approaching the light, Virgil and Dante are reinvigorated. They are eager to keep moving, pushing ahead "to go back to the world of light, / and without any care to rest at ease." Dante experiences some sort of deliverance from sin. A burden has been lifted from his shoulders. He can taste the freedom, and nothing can be allowed to stand in his way.

139 After the claustrophobic darkness of hell, what a great relief to be in the open, to see the stars, to be able to redirect one's sight upwards again, towards the light. Triumph over sin is the only way to true freedom. Sin makes us a smaller sort of thing, limiting our possibilities, hindering our happiness, and impeding our progress to our final goal. Sin makes us slaves.

Dante had entered hell because he had lost his way

in the dark woods. By his experience of hell, by seeing firsthand the destructive power of sin, the emptiness of evil, Dante is ready to face the light. He knows that the only path to happiness is the steep and narrow road. But he is now determined to make the climb.

He hopes his reader is ready as well, because this journey is one that every human soul must make. Life, eternal life, depends upon it.

TAN · BOOKS

TAN Books is the Publisher You Can Trust With Your Faith.

TAN Books was founded in 1967 to preserve the spiritual, intellectual, and liturgical traditions of the Catholic Church. At a critical moment in history TAN kept alive the great classics of the Faith and drew many to the Church. In 2008 TAN was acquired by Saint Benedict Press. Today TAN continues to teach and defend the Faith to a new generation of readers.

TAN publishes more than 600 booklets, Bibles, and books. Popular subject areas include theology and doctrine, prayer and the supernatural, history, biography, and the lives of the saints. TAN's line of educational and homeschooling resources is featured at TANHomeschool.com.

TAN publishes under several imprints, including TAN, Neumann Press, ACS Books, and the Confraternity of the Precious Blood. Sister imprints include Saint Benedict Press, Catholic Courses, and Catholic Scripture Study.

For more information about TAN,
or to request a free catalog, visit
TANBooks.com

Or call us toll-free at
(800) 437-5876

Spread the Faith with . . .

TAN·BOOKS
A Division of Saint Benedict Press, LLC

TAN books are powerful tools for evangelization. They lift the mind to God and change lives. Millions of readers have found in TAN books and booklets an effective way to teach and defend the Faith, soften hearts, and grow in prayer and holiness of life.

Throughout history the faithful have distributed Catholic literature and sacramentals to save souls. St. Francis de Sales passed out his own pamphlets to win back those who had abandoned the Faith. Countless others have distributed the Miraculous Medal to prompt conversions and inspire deeper devotion to God. Our customers use TAN books in that same spirit.

If you have been helped by this or another TAN title, share it with others. Become a TAN Missionary and share our life changing books and booklets with your family, friends and community. We'll help by providing special discounts for books and booklets purchased in quantity for purposes of evangelization. Write or call us for additional details.

TAN Books
Attn: TAN Missionaries Department
PO Box 410487
Charlotte, NC 28241

Toll-free (800) 437-5876
missionaries@TANBooks.com